The Law and Constitution
for Every Jamaican

The Law and Constitution
for Every Jamaican

David Batts

The Caribbean Law
PUBLISHING COMPANY

Kingston • Miami

First published in Jamaica, 2022 by
The Caribbean Law Publishing Company
An imprint of Ian Randle Publishers
16 Herb McKenley Drive
Box 686
Kingston 6
www.ianrandlepublishers.com

© 2022 David Batts
ISBN: 978-976-96283-9-7 (pbk)

National Library of Jamaica Cataloguing-In-Publication Data

Name: Batts, David, author.
Title: The law and constitution for every Jamaican / David Batts.
Description: Kingston : Caribbean Law Publishing Company, 2022.
   lIncludes bibliographical references.
Identifiers: ISBN 9789769623897 (pbk).
Subjects: LCSH: Constitutional law – Jamaica. l Civil rights – Jamaica.
   l Jamaica – Law and legislation. l Due process of law – Jamaica.
Classification: DDC 342 -- dc23.

Cover and Book Design by The Caribbean Law Publishing Company
Cover Illustration: Jiore Z. Moore-Gayle
Printed and Bound in the United States of America

To my parents, George and Clover, without whom I would not have been.

And to the people of Jamaica whose ability to overcome continues to amaze.

Contents

Foreword

The Constitution is the highest law. Every other law must conform to it. If that other law does not, then a court must declare void that part of the other law that contradicts the Constitution.

Among the several things the Constitution does is tell people what their fundamental rights are. It guarantees them the means for protecting and advancing those rights. It establishes the three mighty arms of the state: the Parliament that makes the laws; the government that administers these laws; and the courts that interpret and apply the laws. It outlines the basic obligations people have to one another and to the state, and the obligations the state has to the citizenry. The Constitution further creates important governmental bodies that flesh out and carry forward the aims of the Constitution, and it also gives us the terms of reference of the highest holders of public office. It explains how these institutions and office-holders should conduct themselves and the affairs of the country. It spells out what choices can and cannot be made, whether by them or by the people themselves as a whole.

The workings of the Constitution seriously affect every single Jamaican, every minute of every day. It is, therefore, not enough that only judges and lawyers, parliamentarians, and government officials should understand what is in the Constitution and how it operates. Ideally, every citizen should have a basic understanding of the highest law. Such an understanding would surely lead to better governance because then, not only will everyone know clearly what can and what ought not to be done, it would be easier to hold both the important institutions and those who hold public office to account.

In *The Law and Constitution for Every Jamaican*, Justice Batts successfully embarks upon this ambitious task of enabling such an understanding. He summarises, for the ordinary woman, man, girl, and boy, all the above-mentioned aspects of the law and Constitution of Jamaica. It is a remarkable feat, given its brevity and impressive sweep. In less than two hundred pages, he addresses the main features of the Constitution and the law. Methodically, he goes through each of the ten chapters of the Constitution, explaining in simple language the essence of what each chapter conveys.

Justice Batts was not content merely to describe, however succinctly, the functions of the most important institutions of governance and those of the most important public office-holders. Helpfully, he also sets out the broad context surrounding and shaping the development of the Constitution and the law. To do this, he first gives the reader a flavour of the various legal systems that exist in the world. This places into context the Common Law system we practise. How did we get that system? What are its main features? How does our Common Law system compare to the Civil Law system and to other legal systems? These questions are concisely answered in a way that sufficiently allows a reader to have a better grasp of Jamaica's Independence Constitution.

Of course, the Constitution, introduced in 1962, did not fall from the sky. It may have been drafted in the United Kingdom following discussions among Jamaica's political leaders and with British officials. But what is stated in the Constitution is really the product of the energies of and historical struggles waged by the people of Jamaica for freedom, prosperity, and a life of fulfilment. It is these struggles that have taken Jamaica, like its sister states of the Caribbean Community, on a journey that has resulted in emancipation from enslavement, the formation of trade unions, the right of every adult to vote, the formation of political parties, independence from the colonial yoke, and a Constitution with a charter of fundamental rights to be enjoyed by all. These are significant landmarks on a continuing journey, but there are notable milestones still left to be achieved.

However briefly, Justice Batts captures it all, beginning with the Taínos and their momentous encounters with European adventurists, beginning with those of 'a lost Christopher Columbus [who] stumbled upon the islands of the Caribbean.' At every step of the way, Justice Batts draws the unbreakable link between the struggles of the people of Jamaica and the country's constitutional and legal advancement. This is critical. Too often law is taught in a way that divorces it from, or at least pays insufficient regard to, the underlying social and economic forces that shape the law. Securely closing this gap helps ordinary people to recognise better their worth and potential. It reinforces the truth that it is their sweat and labour, their tears and disappointments, their triumphs and accomplishments that, in the end, play the defining role in constitutional progress. Moreover, a fulsome appreciation of the social, political, and economic interests served by the law can only enhance the process of legal interpretation.

The Law and Constitution for Every Jamaican is written from an uncompromisingly nationalist, anti-colonial perspective. It properly places ordinary Jamaicans at the centre of the events fashioning their destiny. Befitting a book written for the mass of people, Justice Batts writes in plain English, avoiding complex details and legalese. He ends by expressing the hope that every Jamaican will one day understand the rights and duties that go with citizenship, and he suggests that the measure of the book's success is whether it will inspire at least one Jamaican to say, 'I now know and understand my role, obligations and rights.' I venture to suggest that, by this yardstick, the book is sure to be a great success.

The Honourable Mr Justice Adrian Saunders
President
Caribbean Court of Justice

1.
Introduction

Mr Hemans and his family, some of whom were visiting from abroad, went to the very popular Hellshire beach to enjoy fish and festival. It was dark when the two-car convoy left the beach. Mr Hemans was driving the lead vehicle. Upon exiting the beach he was motioned to stop by a uniformed police officer.[1]

He complied with the police officer's request and exited the vehicle. His brother, who had been travelling in the vehicle behind, took objection and asked the officer the reason for the stop and why a search of the vehicle was required. The police officer did not take kindly to this intervention, and his response prompted Mr Hemans to say that it was only the fact that the officer had a gun why he felt emboldened to respond in the way he had to his brother's enquiry. Thereupon the police officer put his weapon aside and proceeded to physically assault Mr Hemans. The beating came to an end only with the intervention of the policeman's colleagues. Mr Hemans was forced into the police service vehicle and taken to the police station where, among other things, he was made to stoop on his haunches nude, in the guard room, which was open to the public.

Sitting as a judge in the Supreme Court of Judicature of Jamaica, and hearing this evidence, what concerned me was the reason advanced for stopping Mr Hemans that day.

The lawyer, from the Attorney General's Department, who represented the police officer said the stop was *in order to conduct a search for guns and drugs*. Mr Hemans had made no claim about the interruption of his freedom of movement.

In that courtroom no one seemed to appreciate that the entire episode would have been avoided had the constitutional rights of Mr Hemans, to go about his lawful business, been respected. It seems neither those charged to uphold the law nor those the subject of the law were aware that a police officer has to have an honestly held suspicion, based on reasonable grounds, prior to interfering with the liberty of any subject. In other words, Mr Hemans should not have been stopped unless there was reasonable cause to believe he had committed, was about to commit or, was in the act of committing some unlawful act or, there was some reason having to do with traffic control or public safety. No reason was given at the time of the incident and none was advanced in court.

Jamaicans have for much of our history been excluded from the mainstream of the social order. The rights, duties, and responsibilities of citizens in a democratic state were not organically generated and therefore have not been culturally passed from one generation to another. The efforts by the state to educate Jamaican citizens about the law and Constitution since political independence of 1962 have been inadequate.

It is this realization, more than any other, which prompted my desire to write. It is my hope that every Jamaican will one day understand the rights and duties that go with citizenship. If this publication causes even one Jamaican to say *I now know and understand my role, obligations and rights,* it will have been a success.

In Jamaica, rarely does a sitting judge publish a book on the law. I am aware that former Justice of Appeal Karl Harrison published two law books while sitting as a judge. The Honourable Kipling Douglas (Ret'd) also has a publication. There have not been many others. In other jurisdictions sitting judges seem to be more active in that regard. Lords Denning and Bingham in England come to mind. Regionally, the Honourable Adrian Saunders, the President of the Caribbean Court of Justice, co-wrote a leading text on constitutional law. By joining this exclusive club, I sincerely hope to encourage other members of the Jamaican judiciary to similarly share their experience, ideas, and knowledge.

This publication explains the development of Jamaican law from earliest recorded history to the present. It looks at our institutions, the role of law in society, how our courts function, human rights, and the responsibilities of the citizen, in a way that all can understand. The detailed notes at the end of the book, should be of great value to anyone wanting to do further research.

I invite you to turn the page and let us together explore Jamaican Law and its Constitution.

2.
The Law and Legal Systems
of the World

Definition of Law

A law is a rule so important that the society attaches legal consequences for its breach. The legal consequence may be a criminal prosecution, a civil lawsuit, or both. Laws are to be distinguished from rules, which have no such consequence if they are breached. So, for example, as a rule we wear a watch on the left hand and if we enter a room and see other persons we say *good morning* or give a cordial greeting. Unlike a law, however, a breach of either of these rules will result in no legal consequence for the offender.

Legal Systems of the World

A body of laws together create a legal system. Each state in the world operates a legal system. Legal systems reflect the legal tradition, or traditions, from which the laws emerged. H. Patrick Glenn, in his renowned work, *Legal Traditions of the World*,[1] identifies the seven major legal traditions from which legal systems emerged as the Chthonic, Talmudic, Civil, Islamic, Common Law, Hindu, and Confucian.

The categories of systems of law in the world today by characteristic features of their content and structure are: the Common Law Legal System, the Civil (or Continental) Legal System, the Socialist (or Communist) Legal System, and the Religious Legal System. A state may have features of more than one of the systems and is then said to have a hybrid legal system.

The Common Law Legal System

The Common Law Legal System originated in, and is identified with, the country we now know as the United Kingdom. The system evolved, over hundreds of years, after the Norman (French) conquest of England in 1066. Today, the Common Law Legal System has two main features. The first is that most of the law is to be found in the decisions of judges (called case law), and the second is the structure of the law-making institution.

Role of Case Law

The prominent role of judges, in the Common Law Legal System, is due to the manner in which law was applied in earlier times in England. England was for a time the dominant state in the United Kingdom, which today comprises England, Wales, Scotland, and Northern Ireland. The English King had judges who would go out on circuit to dispense justice throughout the country. The source of their authority was the writ. Many cases were decided by juries, and the judge's role was to decide on the law. Records were kept of these judicial decisions.

Over time, each decision became a binding precedent so that another similar case would be decided in a similar manner. Judges in this way, it was said, did not make law; they only declared the law. The judges reasoned by analogy to come to their decisions. A hierarchy of courts later developed as appeals were made to a higher court which could bind a lower court even if that lower court's ruling was earlier in time.

In the Common Law Legal System, the decisions of the judges are reported in books called law reports. There are a great many such reports. In order to know what the law is on a subject (or what the court's decision is likely to be in any situation), it is necessary to search through the law reports to find a decided case on similar facts. These are called judicial precedents. Attorneys-at-law are trained to do this research and to utilize such previous decisions to bolster their arguments or to advise their clients.

Bicameral Parliament

The second major identifiable feature of the Common Law Legal System is its law-making institution and how it is structured. The structure has developed over time. Hundreds of years ago England was ruled by a monarch, that is a sovereign (King or Queen), who had absolute law-making power. He (or she) governed by edict. As the society developed the people wanted a greater say in how resources were distributed and in what laws were made. There was a revolution and counter-revolution in England. Eventually, a structure emerged which allowed for the sharing of power between the king and his nobles, on the one hand, and the elected representatives of the people on the other. The Parliament which emerged consisted of:

- A Lower House in which sat the people's elected representatives. It is referred to in England as the House of Commons, while in other places, like Jamaica, it is called the House of Representatives.

- An Upper House in which traditionally sat the nobles or lords, being persons of property and traditional wealth, who represented the king's interests. They were generally regarded as being above the fray of day-to-day politics, and were there to temper the excesses of the Commons. Nowadays, the Upper House in most Common Law Legal Systems is referred to as the Senate. It consists of persons appointed by the leadership on both sides of the Lower House or in some countries of persons representing sectoral interests or elected. A Bill (or draft law) has to be debated and passed in both the Lower and Upper House before becoming law.

- The Monarch. The role of the Monarch, in this law-making process, is to sign into law any Bill which has been passed in both Houses. A Bill does not become a law until signed. It is an unbreakable convention in the Westminster system that the monarch must sign any Bill which has been passed by both Houses of Parliament. The Monarch also plays a ceremonial role at the opening of a Parliamentary session and reads a throne speech written by the person commanding majority support in the House of Commons. That person is referred to as the Prime Minister. The Monarch's role is performed by a President in countries with a Common Law system but which no longer have a Monarch. Those countries are called republics. Guyana, Trinidad and Tobago, Dominica and Barbados are republics in the Caribbean region which have Common Law legal systems. A Governor-General (the Queen's representative) performs the Monarch's functions in Common Law countries, like Jamaica, which retained the British monarch as head of state after independence.

The Common Law Legal System is to be found in many countries around the world because Britain was for centuries an imperial power. It was popularly said to be *'the empire on which the sun never set'* because at some place in the world, at any given time, it was day somewhere in the British Empire. The process of colonization led to the spreading of English laws and tradition and hence the use of the Common Law Legal System.

Subsequent chapters will look more closely at the Common Law Legal System in Jamaica and how it functions today.

The Civil (or Continental) Legal System

The Civil Law legal tradition originated on the continent of Europe. It is therefore also referred to as the Continental Legal System. Many of its laws and practices have their origin in the law of ancient Rome. There was a time when the Roman Empire dominated most of Europe and even parts of England. Roman Law was written or as it is said, *codified*. Centuries later, after the rise of Emperor Napoleon Bonaparte and the expansion of the French Empire, the *Code Napoleon* and the idea of a code of laws spread across Europe. In the Civil Law Legal System, the statute (codified law) is the most popular legal source.

Comparison with the Common Law System

The primary role of the judge in the Continental Legal System is to apply the codified law and not to *declare* law. Civil Law judges place more emphasis on the writings of jurists and academic scholars than do the judges in the Common Law Legal System. Judges in this tradition also function in more of an inquisitorial (H. Patrick Glenn prefers the term *investigative*) role, unlike the Common Law judge, who sees himself as an umpire between contending parties.

Generally, countries with the Continental system do not have much of a role for a civilian jury.[2] So, whereas in the common law courts many cases have a role for ordinary men and women as deciders of fact, the Civil Law tradition tends to rely mainly on trained judges to decide the facts and the law. This may be why continental courts often have more than one judge hearing a case and appeals sometimes take the form of a rehearing in which evidence is taken and considered. In some Civil Law countries the judge hearing the case will sit with two or more assessors to assist with his determination.

There are similarities between the Continental and the Common Law legal systems. Both emphasize the independence of judges and generally have regard for individual rights and the rule of law.

Presence in the Caribbean

Caribbean countries previously colonized by Spain, Portugal, Holland, or France tend to have Continental legal systems. Some Caribbean states were at one time or the other colonized by more than one colonizer and therefore manifest characteristics of more than one legal system. St Lucia, which was finally ceded to England from France in 1814 (Treaty of Paris), is an example. It has the Continental Legal System with strong Common Law influences.[3]

The Socialist Legal System

This system had its genesis in the Russian Revolution of 1917. The Bolshevists led by Vladimir Lenin overthrew the undemocratic Czar (or King) of Russia. The theoretical underpinning of this Bolshevik revolution is found in the teachings of the European sociologists Karl Marx and Friedrich Engels. Essentially, they saw human development as characterized by a struggle between classes in society. It was all about who controlled the means of production and how items produced were to be distributed. The Socialist Legal System has an ideological focus, which sees the role of the state as being to advance the interest of the working classes. The ultimate aim is to create a society without classes in which wealth is distributed '*from each according to his ability to each according to his need.*'[4] At that stage, it is said the society would be communist or communal in nature.

In its purest form the Socialist Legal System places little emphasis on individual rights, which are generally circumscribed for the common good. There is little scope for the private ownership of property because the means of production are owned by the state. There tends to be only one political party, and there is no role for judges who function independently of the government. This is because the judiciary, like all other institutions of the state, exists to advance the interests of the state and its ideological objectives.

Socialist Legal Systems Today

After the First World War, Russia and its satellite states became the Union of Soviet Socialist Republics (USSR). Another Socialist state, the People's Republic of China, emerged after Mao Zedong (Chairman Mao) led a popular and successful revolution. The secularist teachings of Confucius, and the Buddhist religion, were for a time suppressed. Vietnam and Cuba are other countries with socialist legal systems.

In the 1990s, the USSR collapsed or was voluntarily dismantled mainly because its economic system failed. Today, it is debatable whether the Russian legal system is socialist. It is perhaps more accurately categorized as Continental. Today also, China has moved toward an economy encouraging private sector growth and development. There has been a revival of the Confucian approach to legal relations, which is characterized by informality. It remains to be seen whether or how these developments will ultimately impact the operation of China's legal system.

Socialism in the Caribbean

In the Caribbean Cuba operates a Socialist Legal System. The Guyanese Constitution declares Guyana to be a Socialist state; however, its legal system most closely resembles the Common Law and Continental traditions.

The Religious Legal System

In this system, as the name implies, religion shapes and determines the content of law and how it is applied. Holy books, scriptures, and the teachings of prophets determine legal content and even political behaviour. In many countries with this system, a religious leader is the ultimate ruler or head of state. Countries in the Middle East such as Iran and Saudi Arabia operate religious legal systems. In others, such as Nigeria, elements of a religious legal system operate alongside another (in Nigeria's case a Common Law) system.

Conclusion

These, in a nutshell, are the characteristics of the legal systems of the world. If you wish to learn more about them, I would suggest you read, Rose-Marie Belle Antoine's *Commonwealth Caribbean Law & Legal Systems*,[5] or H. Patrick Glenn's *Legal Traditions of the World*.

3.
How Jamaica Received
Its Legal System

Jamaica is an island in the Caribbean Sea. It is one of the four largest islands of the Greater Antilles. The others are Cuba, Hispaniola, and Puerto Rico. Of the four, Jamaica is the only predominantly English-speaking country. Cuba, a former colony of Spain, is Spanish-speaking as is Puerto Rico, which is now a dependency of the United States. Hispaniola consists of two countries, namely French-speaking Haiti (formerly a colony of France) and the Spanish-speaking Dominican Republic (formerly a colony of Spain). They reflect the language, as well as elements of the legal systems, of their colonizers. These islands, geologists tell us, were formed as a result of volcanic activity millions of years ago. This explains Jamaica's major geographical feature, which is, a range of mountains forming the backbone of the island. Its verdant forests, many rivers, and beautiful beaches have been the subject of legend.

The Taínos
Jamaica's original inhabitants were Taínos, nomadic hunter-gatherers and fishers, who came by boat between AD 600 and 900 from the mainland of South America. The history books describe them as more peaceful than the Kalinagos or Caribs, their warlike cousins, who settled in the Eastern Caribbean.

'Arawak,' was the language of the Taíno people. We know little about their laws or legal system, but we know they lived communally, with each group being led by a chief called a cacique.[1] Archaeological research has uncovered artefacts, village sites, and even examples of cave art by these early Jamaicans.[2] The Taínos' way of life would never be the same after 1492 when a lost Christopher Columbus stumbled upon the islands of the Caribbean. He called the area the *Indies* as he thought he was in the east and close to India. In 1494 on a subsequent voyage, Columbus visited Jamaica for the first time and, in 1503, returned to establish its first Spanish settlement.

Columbus, although Genoese,[3] sailed under the flag of Spain, his trip having been sponsored by King Ferdinand and Queen Isabella, the Spanish Monarchs. On seeing the Taínos, Columbus wrote in his journal that *'they ought to be good servants and of good skill,'*[4] and these gentle people of the Greater Antilles were promptly enslaved by the Spaniards. Overwork, brutal suppression of their wars of resistance, and diseases brought by Europeans effectively decimated their population[5] as the pleas of Las Casas (a Roman Catholic priest) and others went unheeded. Although there is evidence that a few survived, by fleeing into the mountainous terrain, the Taínos as a community ceased to exist in Jamaica during the 150 years of Spanish occupation.

Some of the Taínos' cultural and culinary practices survived. The Europeans adopted and popularized the smoking of tobacco and sleeping in a *hammock* (the original Taíno word). Today, Jamaicans prepare and eat grated cassava, called *bammy,* in much the same way as the island's original inhabitants had done so long ago. Indeed, *Jamaica* is thought to be derived from the Spanish *Xaymaca,* itself thought to be a corruption of the original Taíno word *Yamaye,* meaning land of wood and water. Although represented on Jamaica's Coat of Arms, the Taínos' have had no influence on the law and Constitution of Jamaica.

The Spanish

The Spanish did not find the gold they hoped for in Jamaica and so farmed tobacco, cotton, and food crops instead. They also raised cattle and horses. These products were exported to Spain and to other parts of the new Spanish Empire. To replace the decimated Taíno workforce, Africans were imported and enslaved. The population of Jamaica was rather small whilst under Spanish rule.[6]

The island had been gifted to Columbus by the Spanish monarchs and, after his death, was inherited by his son Diego. He in 1509 dispatched a governor, Juan de Esquivel, with instructions to *subdue and colonise* the island. Governor Esquivel maintained law and order by brutally suppressing and enslaving the Taínos. At that time, the Roman Catholic Church was extremely influential and the legal system in place, although Continental, reflected aspects of a Religious Legal System. It was the church which, in an all too late effort to save the Taínos, persuaded the Crown to grant the first *asiento* or permission to import and enslave Africans in 1517.[7]

The English

Spanish rule in Jamaica continued until 1655 when Oliver Cromwell (then the ruler of England, the English Monarchy having been deposed) sent an expedition headed by Admiral Penn and General Venables to capture Hispaniola. The venture failed miserably, but the military commanders, not wishing to return to England empty-handed, set their eyes on the lesser prize of Jamaica. After five years of fighting, the invaders prevailed, and the Spaniards fled the island, leaving empty buildings behind.[8]

With the retreat of the entire population of Spaniards from Jamaica, the Englishmen took control of an island, which had no functioning legal system. The English treated this conquered territory as settled and therefore applied all the laws of England, so far as they were relevant to their circumstances. This, of course, meant that the Common Law Legal System,[9] was applied.

Reception Rules

As colonies were acquired English judges developed principles to determine the law to be applied in their newly acquired territories. These principles, called *reception rules*, were laid out by an English court[10] and are as follows:

(a) Where a colony was settled, that is, where no established *civilized* system was in place, the English settlers brought with them so much of the laws of England as were applicable to their circumstances. The law of England automatically applied until the colony established its own House of Assembly to make laws for itself. Laws made in England after that *reception date* would no longer apply automatically to the colony, but the laws in existence in England prior to that *reception date* continued to apply. The settled colony would, after the reception date, only be bound by Imperial Acts of the British Parliament and not by the ordinary laws of England.

(b) Where a colony was captured or ceded, the law and legal system in place would continue to have effect so long as there was no conflict with fundamental principles of English law. The British Government (Colonial Office) had the power to change this arrangement and could apply the law of England if it so desired.

(c) Where, as in Jamaica, there was conquest/cessation but no existing legal system then the rules applicable to a settled colony applied.

The rules of reception are still relevant today. If there is no statute passed by the Jamaican Parliament with respect to an issue, the court may rely on one which was passed in England prior to the 'reception date.' That date is now 1728.[11]

In 1664 Jamaica set up its own House of Assembly.[12] That colonial parliament thereafter made laws for the peace, order, and good government of the island. Jamaica, under British rule, became a plantation economy. Cattle-rearing and tobacco farming dominated,[13] until the value of sugarcane and its easy cultivation in the tropics was realized.[14]

For the next two hundred years sugar would be king. The labour to drive the process was harvested from Africa and laws were enacted to foster, protect, and enhance the slave-based economy. The Africans were brought to the island as chattels (property), and the legal system in place was designed to maintain that situation. This meant that in 1772 when Lord Mansfield, Lord Chief Justice of England, declared that slavery was unknown to the common law and therefore that the *Black* must be set free, the decision applied only to England.[15]

It did not apply to colonies, like Jamaica, which had made legislative provision for slavery.

The Maroons

When the Spaniards fled Jamaica, they left behind hundreds of Africans they had previously enslaved. These men and women were left with weapons and encouraged to continue the war against the British until a promised Spanish return. This group of freedom fighters took to the hills where they established communities of free Black people and were called Maroons.

The British regarded the existence of free Black communities as subversive of their slave-based society. Therefore, for almost one hundred years, war was waged against the Maroons. The *Maroon Wars* ended with treaties of peace as the British armies and colonial militia failed to defeat them. The Maroon communities constituted a mixture of former slaves of the Spanish and their descendants, descendants of the few surviving Taínos, as well as runaway slaves of the British. In 1739, the first Maroon treaty was signed. It granted a measure of autonomy to the Maroons and allowed for peaceful coexistence. In return the Maroons promised to help defend Jamaica against invaders and to henceforth return any runaway slaves.[16] Nowadays, although still culturally and historically distinct, the Maroons participate in and are subject to Jamaica's law and legal system and are Jamaican. There is a claim to statehood and autonomy by some Maroon communities. However, the legal position is that the Constitution of Jamaica applies to the Maroons as it does to any other Jamaican.[17]

English Constitutional Law

In 1655 the English brought with them, and applied, the Common Law Legal System.[18] In order to appreciate Jamaica's Constitution, its laws and practice, it is therefore necessary to take a brief look at the English constitutional law and principles. In this way we will better understand the law that Jamaica received when the English came.

The United Kingdom today consists of England, Scotland,

Wales, and part of Ireland. The entity came about after many wars, royal unions and treaties. The United Kingdom has never had a single constitutional instrument. Their Constitution is described as comprising all the laws and principles related to how that state is governed. The British Constitution is therefore to be found in statutes, decisions of the court, unwritten conventions, as well as the royal prerogative and the rules surrounding its exercise. Some of the major features of the British constitution are as follows:

Parliamentary Supremacy

The shift from an executive authority (Crown) to an elected Parliament is a study in that society's ability to compromise. Although monarchs lost their lives in the process the ultimate result was a bicameral legislature with a monarch whose consent is required for the passage of any law. The Upper House comprises unelected members, typically being members of the gentry – the *Lords* – and the Lower House comprising the people's elected representatives, the *Commons*. The Parliament is supreme, and hence legislation represents the highest source of law in the United Kingdom.[19]

The Rule of Law

The Bill of Rights is an Act of the British Parliament, passed in 1689, and was a product of the *Glorious Revolution* of 1688–89 when the Roman Catholic King James II was overthrown. He was replaced by his Protestant (Anglican) daughter, Queen Mary. This conflict marked the decided shift away from Catholicism and, eventually, away from a monarch with absolute power. The Magna Carta (1215), Habeas Corpus (1679), and the Human Rights Act (1998) are major documentary sources, which reflect the rule of law and curtailment of arbitrary and absolute power. These laws demonstrate that all persons, whether serf or king, are equally bound by law and also subject to its protection.

Conventions

These are uncodified procedural rules and are usually followed without question. A constitutional crisis would result if a convention was ignored. Some examples: i) That the monarch will sign any Bill into law which has been passed in both Houses of Parliament. ii) The Prime Minister is the leader of the party with either an absolute majority of seats or the person most likely to have majority support in the Commons. iii) Money Bills must originate in the House of Commons.

Judicial Independence

The judiciary has not always been *independent* in the way we understand that term. The King's judges were literally all his and the King's Courts his own. Indeed, for most of English history, the Lord Chancellor, England's senior judge, has sat in the Cabinet. However, it is fair to say that the development of the concepts of the rule of law, individual human rights, and an end to the idea of absolute rule by a monarch, would not have been possible without the existence of a more or less independent judiciary. A real separation of powers, between those who make the law and those who apply it, was attempted when written Constitutions were drafted for the United States of America (after the revolution of 1776) and for those commonwealth states which gained their independence in the 1950s and '60s.

Nowadays, it is generally believed that the rule of law cannot exist in the absence of an independent and impartial judiciary. Judicial review of the conduct of government ministers and officials, has become an important check on the power of the state and its agents.

4.

Constitutional Development and the Road to Independence

The legal system operating in Jamaica after 1655 was English. When Jamaica attained its political independence in 1962 that legal system continued.

This is not unusual. After the American revolutionary war of the 1770s, bringing an end to British rule in that country, the leaders of the newly independent United States of America endeavoured in their written Constitution to mimic key features of the British constitutional framework. Thus they entrenched a separation of powers: that is, the executive power of the President was to be checked and balanced by the Legislature and an independent Judiciary. The aim was to avoid a concentration of power and hence prevent despotism. Paradoxically, although the American revolutionaries largely succeeded in this aim, the British who they purported to emulate did not have that great a separation between the three arms of the state.

In Jamaica, constitutional development occurred in stages. Each developmental stage was marked by conflict: slave revolts, post-emancipation rebellion, and the workers' unrest of the 1930s. It is therefore surprising that notwithstanding the turmoil which caused change, that change when it came often involved no fundamental adjustment to the legal structure. It is regrettable that the process of constitutional creation was not more inclusive.

The Early Years, 1655–1664

In the very early period, during and after Jamaica's conquest by England, Jamaica was administered by a military government. In 1661, the King of England, having been recently restored to power (following the end of Cromwell's Protectorate), appointed a council to prepare a Constitution for the island of Jamaica. He promised,

> that all children of our natural born subjects of England to be born in Jamaica, shall from their respective births be reputed to be and shall be, free denizens of England....[1]

In December 1661 the first civilian Governor, Lord Windsor, was appointed. He brought with him a Royal Commission and Instructions authorizing the creation of an Assembly to make laws and levy monies *provided they be not repugnant to any of our laws of England.*[2] The island was to be administered by a Governor, his advisory council, an elected Assembly and, in each parish, local justices and vestry. For the next two hundred years, that Royal Commission and Instructions formed the constitutional framework for the island.

The Period Sugar Was King, 1664–1834

In 1664 the House of Assembly, the members of which were elected on a very narrow franchise, met for the first time in Jamaica.[3] One of its first laws declared that the laws of England were in force in Jamaica. That Assembly also passed a law saying that any imposition of taxation had to be with the consent of the *Governor, Council and Assembly.* In this way, the Jamaican planter class sought to limit the power of the English Governor, and hence the government of England, to control their business and in particular their financial affairs. This set the basis for tension between the colony and mother country.

In 1675 the English government appointed Governor Carlisle and sent him with instructions to rein in the Jamaican colonists. The Assembly, which was then led by Samuel Long (the Chief Justice of Jamaica), resisted and refused to pass Bills put forward by the Governor. Long was eventually relieved of his position and, along with Col. William Beeston, arrested, charged with treason, and sent to England for trial. The charges were dropped and Long reinstated after an enquiry into the entire matter decided that Jamaica was legally entitled to make its own laws. Jamaica was to be treated like Barbados, a settled, rather than a conquered, colony.[4] In this way, Jamaica peacefully achieved recognition of the principle *no taxation without representation*. This position was endorsed by Lord Mansfield, England's senior judge at that time.[5] It meant that the Jamaican House of Assembly was responsible for passing money bills, and the British government could not tax the Jamaican colonists directly.

Sir Thomas Modyford, Governor of Jamaica (1664–71), said of Jamaica: *Right reason, which is the Common Law of England, is esteemed and of force amongst us, together with Magna Carta and the ancient Statutes of England, so far as they are practicable.*[6]

This right reason, which he said was the common law of England, did not extend to the Africans brought forcibly to the island and who would soon form a majority of the population. Under the law of the colony, those Africans were treated as property to which Magna Carta and *right reason* did not apply.

In the period 1664 to 1849, the Governor of Jamaica was appointed by the government of England. He in turn appointed a Council. That Council exercised advisory, legislative and some judicial functions. Then there was the House of Assembly, elected from among the property owners.

There were two representatives per parish. The Governor had veto power over the Assembly's law-making powers. However he depended on the Assembly to vote supplies (money bills). There was therefore a symbiotic relationship as each depended on the other.

In 1728 the House of Assembly passed an important statute granting *perpetual revenue* to the Crown. This reduced the tension between colony and metropole as the Governor's budget and taxes due to the mother country were fixed. That law also confirmed all local enactments and stated that all laws and statutes in England, as at that date, were received as laws of Jamaica. This move changed Jamaica's reception date from 1664 to 1728.[7] Importantly, the Assembly also passed a law preventing the Governor from removing a judge without the consent of five members of his Council and only after the Crown agreed. It was a first step towards judicial independence in Jamaica.[8] This governmental structure was dominated by the Jamaican plantocracy most, if not all, of whom were White and male. There was no role in the constitutional structure for the other inhabitants of the island, the majority of whom were either women, Jews, free Black and brown Jamaicans (who could not meet the restrictive property requirements) or Africans and descendants of Africans, brought to Jamaica and enslaved.[9]

Emancipation and beyond 1834–1865

The rise and fall of mercantilism is the rise and fall of slavery summarizes the central thesis of Dr Eric Williams's famous work, *Capitalism and Slavery*.[10] The historian and former Prime Minister of Trinidad and Tobago, argued that change to the political structure of the Caribbean colonies occurred due to economic and social pressures. Prime among the social pressures in Jamaica was the change in ratio between White and non-White. In 1677, there were 9,000 White to just over 9,000 Blacks. By 1787, the enslaved numbered 210,894 to 25,000 Whites.[11]

On the economic front the Jamaican planters were, for much of the period, some of the wealthiest people in the world.[12] Great fortunes were made from the sale of sugar. However, by the 1800s, sugar was no longer king. Poor husbandry and agricultural practices resulted in reduced crop yields. The growing free trade movement, (an anti-monopoly lobby), was pushing for removal of the preferential duties sugar enjoyed. This eventually occurred in 1846. British West Indian sugar thereafter faced competition from beet producers, as well as from Cuban and Brazilian large-scale sugar production. The inherent inefficiencies of a slave-based economy were also having an adverse impact on Jamaica. There continued to be many bloody slave revolts, which were always costly to put down and prevent.[13] The imperial government had, in 1776, suffered defeat in the American War of Independence. This had implications for the island's ability to trade and import food. The situation in neighbouring Saint Domingue (modern-day Haiti), where there was a successful revolution in 1804, also proved threatening. That revolution saw the emergence of the first free Black state in the Western world.

The result of all this was that, by the 1800s, there existed in England an increasingly influential movement for the abolition of the slave trade and slavery.[14] Lord Mansfield's declaration in Somerset's case,[15] that the '*black must be set free,*'[16] created added momentum for the anti-slavery movement. It is therefore not surprising that in 1807 the British Parliament, by an Imperial Statute (an Act of the British Parliament that applied to the entire Empire), abolished the slave trade. This cut off the planters' supply of free labour and further complicated the situation of the colonial plantations in the British West Indies.

The Jamaican House of Assembly in 1831 passed a statute increasing civil rights and privileges of free Black and brown men. It gave them the right to vote and hold public office if they satisfied certain property qualifications.[17] The concession was insufficient to stem the tide of change, however, and on August 28, 1833, the British Parliament passed another Imperial Statute abolishing slavery in the British Empire. It is no coincidence that the abolition of slavery came a little over one year after the Christmas Rebellion of 1831 in Jamaica.[18] That revolt was led by Samuel Sharpe who declared before being hanged, '*I would rather die on yonder gallows than live as a slave.*'[19]

After emancipation, the economic and social conditions in Jamaica worsened. Whereas the planters received millions of pounds in compensation from the British Government, for the loss of their property and an extended period of free labour known as the 'apprenticeship system,'[20] the ex-slaves received no compensation whatsoever. Indeed, much of the compensation paid to the planters remained in England where most Jamaican plantation owners resided.[21]

Internal and external pressure for constitutional reform resulted in the Jamaican Assembly passing an Act of 1849, '*For the better government of Jamaica.*' A bi-cameral legislature was created. The new chamber was really the old Governor's Council, but the number of members was increased from twelve to seventeen. They were non-elected. An Executive Committee was created, three members of which were appointed by the Governor from among the Assembly and one from the new Legislative Council. The Governor was provided an Advisory Council which he appointed. The effect, according to Barnett, was to separate legislative and financial power from administrative functions.[22]

In this period, George William Gordon was persuaded to leave the Legislative Council and seek election to the House of Assembly. There this Jamaican, of mixed race, would become a voice for the peasant class. A 'Town Party' emerged in this period which represented the rising middle class of mainly non-White traders. On the other hand, the Country Party supported the White planter class. These were not formal political organizations but were identifiable sectoral groupings. The House of Assembly was therefore divided along class and colour lines. In 1865, Gordon was an elected representative of St Thomas in the East.[23]

In the 1860s the Governor, Edward Eyre, found common cause with the Country Party. He blocked Bills put forward by the Town Party and was generally very critical of those Assemblymen. The Assembly was elected on a very narrow franchise, at that time limited to landowners with a net annual income from land of £150 or £200 partly from land, partly from an office or business, or £300 from office or business, or who paid tax of £10 per year. In 1864, of a population of 500,000 adults, only 1,903 persons were qualified to vote.[24] In 1865 as a result of the poor economic conditions, the exclusion of the majority from political participation, attempts to evict formerly enslaved tenant farmers from land, and an unfair system of justice, an uprising occurred. Economic hardship, injustice, and lack of political representation formed the backdrop for what became known as the Morant Bay Rebellion. The revolt started at the Morant Bay courthouse, which was burnt to the ground. This was significant because the judges were at that time not independent of the planters' interests and therefore did not have the confidence of the majority of the population.

The revolt was brutally suppressed. George William Gordon was taken from Spanish Town to Morant Bay, where

Martial Law had been declared. He was tried, summarily convicted, and hanged. Hundreds of lives were lost, women were raped, and property destroyed in the course of the rebellion and its suppression. The atrocities committed by the British were such that Governor Eyre was summoned to England and tried for misconduct. He was acquitted of any wrongdoing but was not returned to Jamaica.[25]

Crown Colony Government (1866–1944)

In the wake of the rebellion, which some historians now call the Morant Bay War, the House of Assembly voted itself out of existence. Jamaica was therefore relegated to full Crown Colony Government (that is direct rule by the British Government). The planters did this rather than broaden the franchise and give the right to vote to a wider cross section of the society. From 1866 to 1884, Jamaica was run by the Governor and a Legislative Council of twelve members. The Governor appointed and removed Council members virtually at pleasure. He also appointed and removed judicial officers. In this period, there were some positive social and economic initiatives. The system was premised on the idea that non-White people required White governance.[26]

This Crown Colony system of government was modified in the period 1884–1944. There were then four ex officio members of the Legislative Council, five nominated unofficial members, and nine elected members who had to own a lot of property to qualify. The voting franchise was also property-based and restricted. The Governor had the power to frustrate money Bills and could give effect to any Bill, even if not supported by the Council, if he considered it to be important. In 1895, the number of elected representatives was increased from nine to fourteen. According to Barnett,[27] in this system, power was divorced from responsibility. In 1884, of a population of 600,000, only 9,176 were registered to vote. In 1901, of 756,000 people only 16,256 were registered voters. In 1919, the franchise was extended to women, but they too had to satisfy the property qualifications.

Universal Adult Suffrage, and the Road to Independence (1944–1962)[28]

After the First World War (1914–18), and due to inflation, increased numbers attained the franchise. In 1921, of 858,000, as many as 42,267 were registered to vote. A rising middle class of coloured professionals, merchants, and small farmers began to play a greater role in public life in Jamaica. The advocacy of persons like Dr Robert Love (1839–1914) and Marcus Garvey (1887–1940) led to greater political participation and the emergence of an early trade union movement.[29] That development laid the groundwork for agitation by the rural working class and urban port workers as economic conditions worsened. The organization and agitation of the workers, led by St William Grant, Alexander Bustamante, and his cousin Norman Manley, would lead to further constitutional change.

In 1938, one hundred years after emancipation, rebellion, strikes, and discontent spread across Jamaica.[30] In the years that followed, national trade unions and national political parties called for universal adult suffrage and self-government. The British, weakened by two world wars, one of which was still in progress, were in no position to resist fundamental change. A Royal Commission, established by the British Government to investigate the cause of the riots, recommended among other things a limited expansion of the franchise. J. A. G. Smith and the People's National Party (PNP) rejected those limited reforms and pushed for even greater change.

In 1944, therefore, a new Constitution was put in place for Jamaica. In this new arrangement, the members of the legislature were elected based on universal adult suffrage. The Executive Council consisted of elected and appointed members. It was not just advisory but was the principal instrument of policy. Money Bills had to be approved by the Council before being introduced into the Legislative Chamber. The Legislature was bi-cameral, comprising a House of Representatives and a Legislative Council. The Governor could not now enact laws and only had a *reserve power* where *public order, public health or good governance* required it. It was the elected House which had the real authority.[31]

In the first election under universal adult suffrage it was the Jamaica Labour Party (JLP) and the PNP who dominated, with the JLP winning a majority of seats. In the next election of 1949, this situation continued. Independents won only two seats. This two-party dominance continues to be a feature of Jamaica's political system today.

In 1953, in response to demands by the political parties, internal self-government was granted. The Constitution of that year created a system of Ministers appointed from the Legislature. One Minister was designated Chief Minister. The other Ministers were appointed by the Governor on the Chief Minister's recommendation. Subject areas were now by law assigned to the Ministers. A Public Service Commission was established in 1952 to deal with promotion and discipline in the civil service. Further changes were effected in 1956 and 1957. The Chief Minister would now preside over council meetings and the Governor's role in creating policy came to an end.

In 1959 a new Constitution stipulated full internal self-government and a Cabinet, effectively, the system which would be put in place in the Independence Constitution of

1962. The Governor appointed a Premier and this had to be the person best able to command a majority of seats in the House of Representatives. Importantly, this Constitution granted Judges greater security of tenure and they could not be removed except by a process ultimately involving review by the Judicial Committee of the Privy Council. A Judicial Services Commission was established.

This structure accompanied the federal experiment of 1958. In that year Jamaica, and other countries of the English-speaking Caribbean (sometimes called the Commonwealth Caribbean) at British insistence, created a federal structure. The ten islands operated as one country with a federal Parliament and federal Prime Minister. A federal court to hear all appeals was created. The federal structure was however weak, as too much power was retained by individual states, which meant that some leading politicians chose to serve in their national Parliaments rather than in the federal government. The JLP aggressively criticized this Federation of the West Indies.

Independence (1962–the present)[32]

The federal experiment ended when Jamaica withdrew after a majority of its citizens voted against it in a referendum held on September 19, 1961. In July 1962, the British Parliament passed the Jamaica Independence Act. This statute provided that as from Independence Day (August 6, 1962) the United Kingdom would have no responsibility for the government of Jamaica.[33]

The Jamaican Constitution is the second schedule to an Order in Council issued by the Queen pursuant to powers contained in the West Indies Act of April 1962. In this way 300 years (1655–1962) of English political rule over the island of Jamaica came to an end. Apart from a military camp (valued at £2,500,00) and, the balance (of £1,000,000) in the Colonial Development Fund, the British paid no *compensation* to the descendants of Africans brought to Jamaica forcibly.[34] There was no offer of compensation for the wealth extracted or the fact that at the time Jamaica's unemployment rate was 12 per cent and some 40 per cent of Jamaicans were functionally illiterate.[35] There was little attention paid to the fact that Jamaican society, as a result of its colonial experience, was deeply divided along economic, social, and racial lines.[36] Jamaicans were nevertheless euphoric and very proud, when the red, white, and blue of the Union Jack was lowered and the black, green, and gold of Jamaica's flag was raised, just past midnight on August 5, 1962.[37]

The framers of the Constitution rejected the idea of a constituent assembly and, in the rush to independence, made the Constitution a product of a British Order in Council. A committee was established in Jamaica, which, with limited public participation and involvement, gave its recommendations as to the form, structure, and content of the Constitution. Jamaica's representatives took the draft document to England where its final form and content were settled.

Barnett, in his work, *Constitutional Law of Jamaica,* states,

> Yet the basic principles of the Jamaican Constitution are not the result of political plagiarism or a slavish adoption of current constitutional fashions but are rather the product of three centuries of historical development and a deliberate decision to continue the pattern of a constitutional system which had gradually evolved and in the operation of which the country had acquired considerable experience.[38]

The Constitution of 1962, not surprisingly, has a bicameral legislature, and a Cabinet headed by a Prime Minister. The Prime Minister is appointed by the Governor General being the person who commands majority support in the House of Representatives. There is a Judiciary whose independence is protected by entrenchment in the Constitution of provisions related to removal from office and emoluments. There is a clear demarcation in the Constitution of Executive, Legislative, and Judicial functions. It creates Public, Judicial, and Police Services Commissions, all protected by varying degrees of entrenchment in the Constitution. There is a Bill of Rights, which remarkably, had written into it a Savings Law clause. That clause preserves pre-independence laws from constitutional challenge. Its existence provoked an English judge, sitting in the Judicial Committee of the Privy Council, to suggest that there were no new rights created at independence as colonial laws sufficed.[39] The Savings Law clause section 26 (8) read:

> Nothing contained in any law in force immediately before the appointed day shall be held to be inconsistent with any of the provisions of this chapter, and nothing done under the authority of any such law shall be held to be done in contravention of any of these provisions.

Mercifully, this section was repealed when the Constitution was amended in 2011 and a new Charter of Rights inserted. We will see, however, that even after 2011 the effect of some oppressive laws and practices are still preserved.[40] The Savings Law clause of 1962 was supported on the basis that continuity was necessary and that there would have been chaos if all colonial laws were subjected to constitutional challenge.[41] Its existence may also support an argument that in 1962 the drafters of the Constitution were perfectly comfortable with the Westminster system of law and had no desire to increase the people's involvement in public life beyond a vote every five years. Little interest was shown in having the British provide compensation for the economic, social, and political injury meted out to Jamaicans during three centuries of colonial rule.

Conclusion

Jamaica's independence followed 400 years of European plunder. Military invasion, Maroon wars, slave revolts, popular uprisings, and civil disturbance precipitated changes to its system of governance in that period. The Constitution of 1962, however, reflected an almost seamless continuation of the governmental structure previously in place. Barnett argues that some innovations, such as the entrenchment of the position of Leader of the Opposition, demonstrates the existence of a local *grundnorm* in our Constitution. He believes that, the peoples' general acceptance of the Constitution and their ultimate power to change fundamental features by referendum denote the home-grown nature of the Constitution.[42]

The Jamaican people, however, never approved this Constitution by a direct vote. It was drafted by representatives of, and/or persons appointed by, the two political parties. It was done in a rush and with a desire to continue the same structure of governance. There was, perhaps, insufficient regard for the fact that the majority had long been excluded from the governance structure and may well have expected real change to their political, social, and of course, economic circumstances.[43]

5.
Sources of Jamaican Law

It is said that the difference between a lawyer and his client is that, whereas neither may know what the law is, the lawyer knows where to find it. There is some truth to that. It explains why lawyers in training spend a lot of time learning, and practising, legal research. Although the tools used to effect legal research may change (when this author was a student there were no personal computers nor was there an internet), the sources of the law have not changed.

In Jamaica there are five sources of law:

- The Constitution
- Legislation
- Case Law
- Custom
- International Law.

Custom and International law are the least popular of the sources, but as we will see, whereas Custom is declining in importance, International law is only now developing as a source of domestic law.

The Constitution

The Constitution came into effect when Jamaica gained its independence from England in 1962.[1] It is the highest source of law and the one against which all other laws are judged. If a law, from another source, is inconsistent with the Constitution it is said to be unconstitutional. Such a law is null, void, and of no legal effect. The Constitution of Jamaica sets out the fundamental rights and freedoms of Jamaicans. It also establishes the important institutions of the state and outlines how appointments to those institutions are to be made. The Constitution establishes the three arms of the state: the Executive, the Legislative, and the Judicial.

The Executive

The Constitution vests executive authority in Her Majesty,[2] but provides that it may be exercised on her behalf by the Governor-General.[3] The establishment of the Office of the Governor-General is dealt with in Chapter IV of the Constitution. He is appointed by Her Majesty on the advice of the Prime Minister. The Governor-General represents the Queen of Jamaica when she is not in Jamaica. She is also the Queen of England, and lives there. The monarch's role as Queen of Jamaica is legally distinct from her role as Queen of England. The Governor-General has an advisory body known as the Governor-General's Privy Council.[4] He has the power to grant pardons, called the prerogative of mercy, and does so on the advice of his Privy Council.[5]

The Cabinet also forms part of the Executive arm of the state, and its establishment is dealt with in Chapter VI of the Constitution.[6] The Cabinet is the institution responsible for making policy and directs and controls the government of Jamaica. The Cabinet consists of the Prime Minister and the Ministers of Government whom he appoints. The Prime Minister is appointed by the Governor-General being the person who in his opinion is best able to 'command the confidence of a majority of members' of the House of Representatives.

The Executive arm of the state also controls security and the public service and includes among other offices, the Offices of the Attorney General and the Director of Public Prosecutions. The latter official, although appointed by the Governor-General on the advice of the Public Services Commission, is expressly mandated to function independently.[7]

The Legislature

The Legislative arm of the state is dealt with in Chapter V of the Constitution. It is called Parliament and consists of the Queen, the Senate, and the House of Representatives.[8] The Parliament is responsible for making laws for the 'peace, order and good government of Jamaica'. The laws made by Parliament are called statutes or legislation. The Constitution sets out how members of the Parliament are selected. The members of the House of Representatives (sometimes called the Lower House) are elected.[9] The members of the Senate (sometimes called the Upper House) are all appointed.[10] Thirteen Senators are appointed by the Governor-General, on the advice of the Prime Minister, while eight are appointed on the advice of the Leader of the Opposition.

The Office of Leader of the Opposition is dealt with in Chapter VI, suggesting it is part of the Executive. This may be because the Leader of the Opposition is appointed by the Governor-General,[11] and has a role in the appointment of some public officials, because he has to be consulted.[12] The Constitution does not otherwise define the role of the Leader of the Opposition.[13] However, it is clear that he is a part of the legislature and marshals the viewpoints of those who do not support the government.[14]

A Bill (draft legislation) passed into law by both Houses of Parliament does not become law until the monarch, or her representative the Governor-General, signs it and in that way gives assent. The respective appointments to the Senate are such that, regardless of the majority existing in the House of Representatives at any one time, the majority vote necessary to effect a constitutional change to an entrenched provision,[15] cannot be obtained unless at least one opposition Senator votes in favour of the amendment or a referendum is held. In this way, the Constitution protects against potential tyranny by a majority in Parliament against the minority.

The Judiciary

This arm of the state is dealt with in Chapter VII of the Constitution which states there shall be a Supreme Court and a Court of Appeal. It outlines the method of appointment of the Judges and gives them security of tenure.[16] The provisions mean that a Judge should be able to do his job without having any fear of reprisal, by way of dismissal or salary reduction, from the government or anyone else. Save for the Chief Justice and the President of the Court of Appeal, the Judges are appointed by the Governor-General on the advice of the Judicial Services Commission. The two excepted offices are appointed by the Governor-General on the advice of the Prime Minister after consultation with the Leader of the Opposition.[17]

The Separation of Powers

There is a separation of power between each of these three arms of the state. The courts have decided that the Legislative and Executive arms cannot lawfully, unless there is a constitutional amendment, interfere with the functions of the Judicial arm. Therefore when the Legislature attempted to give the Executive the power, to decide on the sentence of convicted persons, the court decided it was unconstitutional.[18]

The Constitution outlines the way in which it can be amended.[19] Constitutional provisions are either entrenched or unentrenched. Entrenched provisions fall into one of two categories either ordinarily entrenched or deeply entrenched. Ordinary entrenchment means the parliamentary vote must attain a required majority (normally two thirds in each House of Parliament). Deeply entrenched provisions must have a required majority vote in each House of Parliament, and the proposed change must also be put to the people in a referendum. Unentrenched provisions may be amended by a simple majority vote in each House of Parliament. In all cases, whether a provision is entrenched or unentrenched, the Bill[20] proposing the amendment must bear a particular title[21] and must be laid in Parliament by giving a specified minimum time period for its consideration and debate.[22]

The Constitution is the highest law and, as the Constitution creates a Judiciary to interpret and apply the law, it is for the Judiciary to interpret and apply the Constitution.[23] The Constitution of Jamaica gives the Judiciary the responsibility to interpret and apply the Constitution by express provisions.[24]

We will look in greater detail at the Constitution, our highest and most important source of law, in chapters 5 and 6.

Legislation

This is the second highest source of law. Legislation is made by Parliament. In order to create legislation, a Bill, which is a draft of the intended legislation, has to be generated. The Bill is normally created by a Minister of government on the instructions of the Cabinet. It is however possible for any individual Member of Parliament to present a Bill to Parliament. In order to become law, the Bill must be passed by majority vote in both Houses of Parliament and signed by the Governor-General. In the course of passage through the Houses of Parliament, a Bill may undergo several amendments.

The Speaker of the House, who is also a Member of Parliament, controls the procedure in Parliament. He does so in accordance with Parliamentary rules and is not above the law. Therefore on one occasion, when in breach of the Constitution, the Speaker of the House in Dominica refused to swear in the elected Leader of the Opposition, the court ordered him to do so.[25] The court, in recognition of the separation of powers, will refrain from adjudicating on issues concerned only with the internal working of Parliament.[26]

Once it becomes law the Bill is called an Act of Parliament, which is also referred to as statute or legislation. In countries like England, where there is no written Constitution, legislation is the highest source of law. In Jamaica the Constitution is supreme so the legislation that Parliament passes must be consistent with the constitutional provisions. If it is not the court, on an application by affected parties, will strike down the legislation or parts of it.[27]

Legislation, once passed, is enforced by the Executive arm of the state. However, it is the role and function of the Judicial arm of the state to interpret the law and that includes legislation. Judges conduct trials and hear applications, and it is in the course of conducting such proceedings that a Judge will give meaning and effect to legislation. In doing so, the Judiciary utilizes one or other of three rules of statutory construction. These rules are known as the Literal, Golden, and Mischief Rules (sometimes called the Rule in Heydon's case).

The literal rule as the name implies means that the Judge adopts the clear and obvious meaning of the statute. Sometimes a Judge will simply refer to the Oxford English dictionary. The golden rule on the other hand requires a Judge to look beyond a literal interpretation should the literal approach lead to an absurdity. In such a situation, the provision is interpreted so as to avoid an absurd result. The Judge may do this by either implying, or ignoring, words in the statute. The mischief rule is a variation of the golden rule. This approach, popularized in Heydon's case, requires a Judge to ask himself what was the true intent of Parliament and to so construe the law as to advance that intent.[28] There is some tension between the rules, mainly because the traditional approach is to look only at the words of the statute to determine their meaning.[29] It is felt that reference to outside sources, such as the debate in Parliament, is generally unhelpful. This is because the debate will reflect the views of members individually and may not reflect the views of Parliament as a whole.[30]

Case Law (and Equity)

Case Law is the third highest source of law and is found in the decisions of judges. Legislation can therefore overturn or change the effects of a judicial decision in any given case. Case Law is however the most abundant source of law in Jamaica. It is to be found in the reports of judicial decisions. These are called law reports.[31] In trying to find out what is the law on any given subject, lawyers will often try to find a decided case on that subject by looking in the law reports. They will then read the decision of the judge in order to glean from it the applicable law. Lawyers therefore reason by analogy because when arguing a point of law, they reference previously decided cases with similar, or analogous, facts. Even though more and more legislation is passed each year, since it is the Judge who interprets legislation, Case Law continues to be a very important source of law.

Equity

In England, many centuries ago, the King's court (sometimes referred to as the common law courts) developed very complicated and inflexible rules of procedure and practice. This often resulted in injustice mainly because the ordinary man often could not afford the lawyers who were masters of the rules of procedure and pleading. As a result litigants would go to the Lord Chancellor's court[32] and seek relief. The Lord Chancellor developed rules of equity in order to ameliorate the strictures of the common law. So, for example, the King's Court may have dismissed a case because a contract was unsigned even though one party had received the benefit of the contract. The court of equity, in appropriate circumstances, would *treat as done that which ought to be done* for the purpose of enabling the innocent party to sue for payment. The Chancery Court (as the courts of equity were known) over time developed certain forms of relief, such as the injunction, and principles such as estoppel and the constructive trust.[33] Jamaica received, adopted, and applied these principles of equity as part of the Common Law Legal System.

Nowadays, the citizen does not need to go to the court of Chancery to have principles of equity applied. This is because by statute the courts of common law and the courts of equity are fused.[34] In other words, equitable principles are now applied by all judges in all courts.

Case Law, as a source of law, contains both legal and equitable principles.

Law Reporting

In Jamaica, as in most of the Common Law world, the decisions made by courts in the higher judiciary are recorded. Decisions in the civil court are in the form of written reasons for decision called judgments. In cases concerned with the criminal law, judgments are most often recorded at the appellate level. The recording of these judgments is by a process of law reporting. The judgments are edited for grammatical errors and published with indices. Jamaica's system of law reporting is underfunded and in consequence not up to date. Jamaican lawyers therefore rely heavily on law reports from England, Australia, and other common law countries. With the advent of the internet, it is however possible to access, unedited and unindexed, judgments of Jamaican courts by visiting the websites of the Supreme Court and the Court of Appeal of Jamaica.[35]

Binding Precedent

The courts, over time, developed rules related to the application of Case Law. Some of these rules are expressed in Latin so that *stare decisis* (let the decision stand) is important to a system of binding precedent. The earlier decision on a point of law will bind a later court of equal or lower rank, considering the same point of law.[36] In order to identify the binding part of an earlier decision it is necessary to determine the *ratio decidendi* (reasons for decision) of that case. It is not always easy to determine the ratio of a Judgment. A Judge may write 3,000 words in coming to his decision and yet the binding part, the real reason for it, is only expressed in 10 words or less. It is a part of the training of a lawyer to locate and identify the *ratio decidendi* of a case. A judgment may contain a pronouncement on the law, which is not part of the ratio, but is considered authoritative, and hence will be followed, because it was well considered. This is referred to as a *per curiam* declaration or pronouncement. On the other hand, a court may make a decision, or give a judgment, which omitted to consider a statute or earlier relevant and binding case. In such a situation, the judgment is said to be *per incuriam* and will not be considered as a binding precedent.

The UK Privy Council

Jamaica (as well as most Common Law countries) has a hierarchy of courts. Just as earlier decisions bind a court so too do decisions of a higher court bind a lower court. The Jamaican system of courts can be represented as a pyramid. At its apex is the Judicial Committee of the Privy Council (the Privy Council). This court is located in England and is staffed primarily by English judges. It has existed as an institution for over 300 years and originated as a body charged with advising the British monarch. The Privy Council heard appeals from cases decided by courts in all parts of the British Empire. It therefore had a unifying influence on the British Empire.[37] The Privy Council also advised the monarch on other matters, such as, ecclesiastical (church-related) issues.

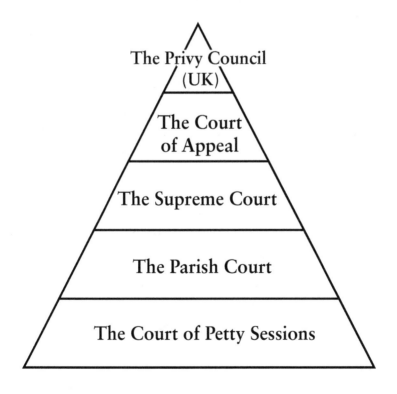

In 1833, the British Parliament passed a law rationalizing the structure of the Privy Council. Since then it has been staffed only by judges who also sit in the English Supreme Court (formerly known as the House of Lords). Provision has been made for judges from countries which continue to utilize that body as their final court, to also sit in the Privy Council. In more modern times, the Chief Justice of Trinidad and Tobago, Sir Hugh Wooding (1966) and Chief Justice Edward Zacca of Jamaica (1992) have been invited to sit there. The occasions were, and are, however quite rare. In the Privy Council, five Judges sit to hear appeals. Although the sitting takes place in England, the national flag of the country from which the appeal originates is displayed in court whenever an appeal from that country is being heard. Lawyers appearing before the Privy Council are entitled to attire themselves in the mode of dress applicable to the country from which the appeal originates or to wear business suits with the consent of the court.

The Court of Appeal

The Court of Appeal is the court immediately below the apex of Jamaica's judicial structure. This court is entrenched,[38] within the Constitution so that its existence, as well as the security of tenure of its members, are protected by the Constitution. Three judges ordinarily sit to hear appeals in this court, which has jurisdiction over all cases, civil as well as criminal, from lower courts. Appeals from the Court of Appeal go to the Judicial Committee of the Privy Council.

The Supreme Court

Below the Court of Appeal is the Supreme Court of Judicature of Jamaica. This court is entrenched in the Constitution and its members' tenure and salary are similarly protected by entrenchment. The Supreme Court is bound by decisions of the Court of Appeal and also by decisions of the Judicial Committee of the Privy Council emanating from Jamaica. In that sense the Supreme Court of Jamaica is not supreme. It is sometimes referred to as our High Court. That it certainly is.

The Supreme Court has two main divisions,[39] a civil division and a criminal division. This is because all law in a Common Law Legal System is either criminal or civil.[40] In its civil division, the Supreme Court has unlimited jurisdiction to decide lawsuits of any value. Issues of commercial law, negligence, family law, matrimonial property, and any matter of dispute between citizens are considered. A single judge sitting without a jury normally hears civil cases. The civil division also hears constitutional questions. These generally are heard by a Full Court consisting of three Supreme Court Judges sitting together.

The other division of the Supreme Court is its criminal division. Here, the Supreme Court sits as a trial court for major criminal offences such as treason, murder, rape, arson, burglary, and those committed with illegal firearms. Most criminal cases in the Supreme Court are heard by a judge and jury. However, cases in its Gun Court division are heard by a judge alone. In some cases, parties, who have a right to trial by jury, may elect to be tried by a judge alone.[41]

The Supreme Court, in both criminal and civil divisions, mostly sits as a court of first instance (that is as a trial court) but does hear appeals from the Courts of Petty Sessions. Supreme Court Judges are, as with judges in the Court of Appeal and the Privy Council, addressed in court as '*My Lord*' or '*My Lady*' as the case may be.

The Parish Court

The Parish Courts fall below the Supreme Court in this triangular judicial design. Parish Courts were, until recently, known as Resident Magistrates Courts.[42] Each parish in Jamaica has its own such court which handles cases concerning issues within the parish. These courts do the bulk of the work in the legal system. It is a trial court with a limited jurisdiction but handles certain serious criminal offences such as fraud and offences under the Dangerous Drugs Act. The jurisdiction has been increased from time to time and, at the date of this publication, Parish Courts hear civil cases concerning claims of a value of $1 million or less. In criminal matters the sentencing power tends to be limited, with most offences carrying no more than a five-year sentence.

Appeals from the Parish Court go to the Court of Appeal. Parish Court Judges are addressed as '*Your Honour.*'[43]

The Court of Petty Sessions

The Petty Session, or Justice of the Peace Court, is the lowest court in the land. This court may be staffed either by two or three Justices of the Peace sitting together or, by a Parish Judge sitting alone. The court of Petty Sessions hears minor criminal cases and also has limited sentencing power, normally, 30 days' imprisonment or less. Justices in Petty Sessions are addressed as 'Your Worship'. Usually they are not legally trained. Justices of the Peace are appointed by the Governor-General from among persons of integrity in the society.[44]

Appeals from decisions of the Court of Petty Sessions are heard by a Supreme Court Judge sitting in chambers.

Courts of Record

The Supreme Court, the Court of Appeal, and the Judicial Committee of the Privy Council are referred to as Courts of Record. This means their decisions constitute binding precedent for the purpose of determining Case Law in the country. There are large numbers of such decisions and hence Case Law, as a source of law, is complex and bulky. Insofar as it depends on decisions of judges there is some flexibility, which sometimes allows for judicial activism. This allowed a new civil wrong (tort) to be developed in the twentieth century when the English House of Lords allowed someone to bring a claim in negligence.[45] Also, in the twentieth century, the *Mareva*[46] injunction was first utilized to allow for pre-judgment injunctive relief.

Case law, as a source of law, suffers disadvantages in that it is not user friendly because of its complexity and the sheer number of cases. It also can be inflexible because of the binding nature of precedent.

Custom

This is the fourth ranked source of law in Jamaica's Common Law Legal System. If there is no applicable constitutional provision, statute, or decided case, a party may attempt to claim a remedy based upon a long practice that has become law. This sometimes occurs in the context of rights to water or the right to passage over land. Custom must not however be confused with prescriptive rights created by legislation. Customary rights refer to those rights that accrue in the absence of any relevant statutory provision.

Rules have been developed in relation to how customary rights are established. The first rule is that the alleged custom must have existed since antiquity. English case law establishes that this must be since the year 1189. Clearly, as Europeans only arrived in Jamaica in 1494, there may be an evidential problem here. The practice, to be a custom, must also have been continually exercised or recognized. There must be no point at which it was interrupted since antiquity. The Custom must have been peacefully practised, be regarded by all as mandatory, and it must not exist due to the licence or permission of anyone. The Customary terms must be certain and consistent with no doubt of its meaning or how far it extends. The Custom, to be recognized as such, must be reasonable. As the lowest source of law it cannot be inconsistent with any provision of the Constitution, Legislation, or Case Law.

These being the prerequisites at Common Law, to establish or identify a Customary Law, it is not surprising that in Jamaica no Customary Law has yet been declared.[47] In *Mitchell v Cowie*[48] the Court of Appeal of Trinidad and Tobago decided that a 'chattel house' formed part of the land and was a fixture for the purpose of giving effect to a transfer of the tenancy. The result was that the person to whom the 'chattel house' was sold acquired no interest in it. The court left open the possibility that, as between a landlord and his tenant, custom and usage may allow for removal of the 'chattel house' upon the tenancy being determined.[49] Here in Jamaica there is often reference to *family land,*[50] which has deep meaning to a great many people, but it is as yet unrecognized in our law.

International Law/Conventions

International Law is sometimes called the law of nations.[51] It consists of those laws binding states in their relations with each other. It is to be found in treaties, international custom, general principles of law, judicial decisions, and teachings of the most highly qualified publicists.[52]

In Jamaica, International Law usually has no force or binding effect within the country and hence is not generally regarded as a source of Jamaican law. The international norm has to be legislated by Parliament in order to become part of domestic law. In modern times, however, courts have, by adapting the principle of *legitimate expectation*, given effect to international legal norms within a country.[53] With the Charter of Rights[54] in 2011 adopting the standard of '*a free and democratic society,*' it is arguable that international law and standards relative to human rights may have a more direct impact on domestic law.

Conclusion

Having reviewed Jamaica's system of law, how it was received, and, the sources of law within that system, chapter 6 explores Jamaica's highest source of law, the Constitution.

6.
The Constitution of Jamaica

The Constitution of Jamaica is the second schedule to an Order in Council made at Buckingham Palace in London, England on July 23, 1962.[1] It is the highest source of law in Jamaica and outlines the structure of government, how laws are made, and how they are enforced. The Constitution also details the fundamental rights and freedoms of all Jamaicans. It is divided into ten chapters, and each chapter has several parts.

Chapter I (Sections 1 and 2) – Preliminary

This Chapter contains the definition of several terms used in the Constitution. It also explains how certain aspects of the Constitution are to be treated. Section 1(9) reads:

> No provision of this Constitution that any person or authority shall not be subject to the direction or control of any other person or authority in exercising any functions under this Constitution shall be construed as precluding a court from exercising jurisdiction in relation to any question whether that person or authority has performed those functions in accordance with this Constitution or any other law.

This provision expressly preserves the power of the courts to review the conduct of persons purporting to act under power given by the Constitution, that is, to ensure that functionaries act within the power granted by the Constitution (intra vires) and not in excess of that power (ultra vires). A functionary will act ultra vires if he does any of the following:

a. ignores any required formalities, for example, if a hearing was required but he failed to conduct one; or

b. if he acts so unreasonably that no reasonable functionary in his position would have so acted; or

c. if he acts unlawfully in the sense that he makes an error of law by, for example, misinterpreting a Constitutional or statutory provision, or

d. acts for an improper purpose or for bad or wrong reasons.

The power of judicial review, expressly preserved by our Constitution, has been exercised by common law courts for a very long

The Power of Judicial Review Expressly Preserved

time. The express statement of the power in the Constitution gives it added import, and arguably increases the power of the court in that regard.[2] Jamaican courts have, on the application of affected persons, reviewed the actions of public functionaries for being ultra vires.[3]

Section 2 of the Constitution provides:

Subject to the provisions of sections 49 and 50 of this Constitution, if any other law is inconsistent with this Constitution, this Constitution shall prevail and the other law shall to the extent of the inconsistency be void.

Chapter I therefore unequivocally establishes that the Constitution is the supreme law of Jamaica against which all other laws may be judged. This provision means that an Act of Parliament will be void if it is inconsistent with the Constitution. The Judiciary is the arm of the state empowered to say when an Act is unconstitutional. Jamaican courts have had cause to do this on more than one occasion since independence.[4]

Chapter II (Sections 3–12) – Citizenship

This chapter treats with the issue of citizenship and defines who is a Jamaican and how citizenship may be acquired. Every person born in Jamaica whether before or after Independence Day (August 6, 1962) is a Jamaican citizen. Citizenship may also be acquired by virtue of parentage. It is also possible for a non-Jamaican to apply to be registered as a Jamaican citizen. Any person deprived of citizenship is given a right of access to the Supreme Court of Judicature of Jamaica to have the decision reviewed. It is possible for a Jamaican to have dual citizenship, that is, to be a citizen of more than one country.

> *...defines who is a Jamaican and how citizenship may be acquired.*

Chapter III (Sections 13–20) – Fundamental Rights and Freedoms

Chapter III contains the Fundamental Rights and Freedoms of all persons under the Queen's peace or, in layman's terms, all persons in Jamaica. The chapter was fundamentally restructured in the year 2011. Unlike the document created in 1962, the 2011 Charter of Rights is written in simple understandable terms. The new statement of rights repealed the savings law clause which, in the 1962 version, immunized pre-independence law from constitutional challenge.

> *...Fundamental Rights and Freedoms...*

The guaranteed rights are to:

- Life, liberty and the security of the person (section 13(3)(a)).

- Freedom of thought, conscience, belief and observance of political doctrines (section 13(3)(b)).

- Freedom of expression (section 13(3)(c)).

- Seek, receive, distribute or disseminate information, opinions and ideas through any media (section 13(3)(d)).

- Peaceful assembly and association (section 13(3)(e)).

- Freedom of movement – the right of every Jamaican to enter Jamaica and of every person lawfully in Jamaica to move around freely throughout Jamaica and to leave Jamaica (section 13(3)(f)).

- Equality before the law (section (13(3)(g)).

- Equitable and humane treatment (section 13(3)(h)).

- Freedom from discrimination on grounds of sex (meaning whether male or female), race, place of origin, social class, colour, religion, or political opinion (section 13(3)(i)).

- Protection from search of person and property, respect for private and family life, privacy of home and privacy of communication (section 13(3)(j)).

- Right of the child to protection as a minor and if a citizen to publicly funded tuition at the primary and pre-primary levels (section 13(3)(k)).

- Right to a healthy environment free from abuse or ecological degradation (section 13(3)(l)).

- Right, if qualified, to register as an elector and to vote in free and fair elections (section 13(3)(m)).

- Right to be granted a passport and not to be denied it except by due process of law (section 13 (3)(n)).

- Protection from torture or inhuman or degrading treatment (sections 13 (3)(o) and 13(6) and (7)).

- Freedom of the person (sections 13 (3)(p) and section 14).

- Protection of property rights (section 13 (3)(q) and section 15).

- Due process (section 13 (3)(r) and section 16).

- Freedom of religion (section 13 (3)(s) and section 17).

The rights provisions are generally subject to the rights of others not to be affected by one person's exercise of his or her rights.[5] The provisions bind not only the state but other persons, natural and juristic.[6] This means a company damaging the environment, for example, may be liable for breach of constitutional rights. The new Bill of Rights specifically exempts the death sentence from being challenged on the grounds of being cruel and inhumane and also because of time served awaiting execution or the conditions of incarceration pending execution. The new Bill of Rights protects from constitutional challenge laws relating to sexual offences or obscene publications or offences related to the life of the unborn.[7]

Sections 14 to 20 of Chapter III flesh out the detailed rights and should be read if their full implications, and limitations, are to be correctly understood. Chapter III also gives the Supreme Court of Jamaica power to hear and determine cases involving allegations of rights abuse.[8]

Chapter IV (sections 27–33)
– The Governor-General

...establishes the office of Governor-General.... outlines how the Governor-General is to go about exercising his functions.

This chapter establishes the Office of Governor-General. This person is the representative of the monarch in Jamaica. Section 32 is located in this Chapter and outlines how the Governor-General is to go about exercising his functions. It distinguishes between functions he carries out on the advice of the Cabinet or a Minister, functions he carries out after consultation and, those in his sole discretion.

The Governor-General is appointed by the monarch on the advice of the Prime Minister.

Chapter V (sections 34–67)
– Parliament

...establishes the Parliament of Jamaica.

This Chapter establishes the Parliament of Jamaica. Parliament consists of Her Majesty, the Senate, and the House of Representatives.

The Senate has 21 members known as Senators, 13 of whom are appointed by the Governor-General on the advice of the Prime Minister. The remaining 8 are appointed by the Governor-General on the advice of the Leader of the Opposition. Those numbers are not random. They ensure that a party in power will not have two-thirds majority of senators appointed by that party. This impacts directly the power of any government to make fundamental changes to the Constitution unilaterally.

The members of the House of Representatives are elected by the people. They are known as Members of Parliament.

Chapter V details qualifications of those entitled to vote, as well as of those who wish to be elected to the House of Representatives.

This Chapter also details the circumstances that may result in the removal of Senators and members of the House of Representatives. They enjoy security of tenure and therefore are not easily removed once appointed or elected. This enables Members of Parliament to fearlessly represent the interests of their constituents. Jamaican courts have pronounced on the security of tenure of Members of Parliament, as well as the qualifications to become a Member of Parliament.[9]

Part 2 of Chapter V sets out the power of Parliament to make laws for the *peace, order and good government* of Jamaica. In carrying out this function, the members of both Houses enjoy certain privileges and immunities. For example, the Constitution precludes any civil or criminal proceeding against any Member of Parliament for words spoken or written in the House or in a report to the House of which he is a member or to any committee of that House. This is called parliamentary privilege, and it is absolute.[10]

Section 49 falls within Chapter V. It is a most important provision because it sets out the levels of entrenchment of Constitutional provisions.

> *Section 49 falls within Chapter V. It is a most important provision because it sets out the levels of entrenchment of Constitutional provisions.*

Parliament may only amend the Constitution in accordance with its provisions. A simple majority can amend any provision unless section 49 says otherwise. That section lists the provisions of the Constitution requiring special majorities in Parliament before they can be amended. Section 49 specifies those sections that require a referendum in addition to, or in lieu of a special majority.

Section 49 is necessary to prevent a tyranny of the majority in Parliament over the minority. Fundamental constitutional change requires more than just a simple or bare majority vote in the Houses of Parliament. In order to make fundamental constitutional change there will have to be cooperation of some members of the Opposition and/or, a vote of the people in a referendum.

Chapter V also has detailed provisions governing the introduction of Bills into Parliament, its rules and how they may be created. It also deals with the process by which constituencies are delineated.

Chapter VI (sections 68–96) – Executive Powers

Executive Authority
- *Governor-General appoints Prime Minister*
- *Cabinet*
- *Attorney-General – government's legal adviser*
- *Leader of the Opposition*
- *Secretary to the Cabinet*
- *Director of Public Prosecutions*

Chapter VI speaks to the executive authority in Jamaica. This is legally vested in *Her Majesty*, the sovereign, but it is a legal fiction. The real power and authority reside in the Cabinet, which formulates government policy. The Cabinet, itself collectively responsible to Parliament, is established in this chapter and forms part of the Executive.

It is the Governor-General who appoints the Prime Minister being the person who, in the Governor-General's judgment, is best able to command a majority in the House of Representatives. The Prime Minister once appointed will thereafter advise the Governor-General whom to appoint as Ministers in the Cabinet.[11] Ministers are selected from among the membership of both the Senate and the House of Representatives. The security of tenure of the Prime Minister and the Ministers is also outlined in this Chapter. A majority in the House of Representatives may vote to revoke the Prime Minister's appointment. That body may also, by majority, vote for a resolution of no confidence in the government and thereby cause the Governor-General to dissolve Parliament. Conversely, the Governor-General exercises the power to dissolve Parliament and call a general election on the advice of the Prime Minister.[12]

Section 79 of Chapter VI, establishes the Office of Attorney-General, the principal legal adviser to the Government. The Office of Leader of the Opposition is created by section 80. He is appointed by the Governor-General being the person best able to command a majority of those in the House of Representatives who do not support the government. The positions of Secretary to the Cabinet and the Office of the Director of Public Prosecutions are also established in this chapter. The Director of Public Prosecutions enjoys security of tenure and constitutional protection of his/her emoluments.

The Governor-General's Privy Council is also found in this Chapter. He makes the appointment to that body after consultation with the Prime Minister. The power to grant pardons for offences is conferred on the Governor-General in this Chapter.

Chapter VII (sections 97–113)
– The Judiciary

This chapter is concerned with the Judiciary. It creates a Supreme Court with a Chief Justice and a Senior Puisne Judge at the helm. The other judges are called Puisne Judges. Puisne (pronounced 'pu-nee') is an old French term which loosely translates to 'younger' and is used with reference to Judges

- *The Supreme Court* of the Supreme Court other than the Chief Justice. The Supreme Court is a court of original jurisdiction, that is, it does mainly trials, not appeals.

- *Court of Appeal* This Chapter also creates a Court of Appeal to which cases from the Supreme Court may go. Three Justices of Appeal sit together to hear appeals. There is a President of the Court of Appeal. The Chapter details the method by which all these judges

- *The Judicial Services Commission* are appointed. It creates an independent Judicial Services Commission for that purpose and protects their remuneration. It also prevents the Parliament or anyone else from abolishing the court or the job of judge whilst there is a holder. The Judges of the Supreme Court and Court of Appeal are protected by constitutional entrenchment of these provisions so that, in accordance with section 49, a special majority is required before they may be amended.

Chapter VII recognizes the continuation of appeals to Her Majesty's Judicial Committee of the Privy Council in England (the Privy Council).[13] Importantly this provision is not entrenched because the framers of the Constitution recognized it would be unwise to entrench a court over whose continued existence Jamaica had no control. It may also have been because they expected that Jamaica would one day soon want to detach itself from that colonial appendage.[14]

Chapter VIII (sections 114–122) – Finance

This Chapter establishes a consolidated Fund for Independent Jamaica. It is here that all government's revenue goes. The Chapter sets out the duties of the Minister of Finance[15] as it relates to the annual budgeting exercise. It also

• *The Consolidated Fund*
• *Minister of Finance*
• *Auditor-General – the overseer of government's accounts*

establishes the office of Auditor-General of Jamaica. The security of tenure of the Auditor-General is also protected by constitutional entrenchment of that position. The Auditor-General cannot be removed from office except by way of an elaborate process. The Auditor-General oversees the accounts of all government departments.

Chapter IX (sections 123–134) – The Public Service

The Public Service Commission is established under this Chapter. It is a body created to handle appointments to the public sector and the removal from employment of persons in the public sector. The Constitution outlines how members of the commission are to be selected for appointment. Once appointed, the Constitution limits the ways in which they may be removed. They too have a measure of Constitutional protection.

• *The Public Service Commission*
• *The Police Services Commission*

This Chapter also establishes a Police Services Commission. Its members are similarly protected and it has similar powers in relation to the police force as the Public Services Commission has in relation to the public (or Civil) Service.

This Chapter also addresses the question of public sector pensions.

Chapter X (sections 135–138) – Miscellaneous

The final Chapter is very short and deals with certain miscellaneous matters. It deals, for example, with how rules are to be made regulating the procedure of commissions appointed under the Constitution. It seeks to prevent the question of the validity of acts of members of those commissions being enquired into by the Courts.[16]

Conclusion

These then are the ten Chapters of our Constitution. You should now be able to quickly find the details of your rights and the obligations of public servants.

7.

The Trial Process

A trial is one method by which legal issues are resolved. A legal issue falls into either one of two broad categories, it is either criminal or civil. There are therefore two major categories of trial, civil, and criminal. The category indicates: (a) the type of court involved, (b) the procedure to be used in that court and, (c) the results which can be achieved.

Although a law is either criminal or civil, the same activity can constitute a breach of both the criminal and the civil law. So that, a motorist who exceeds the speed limit and has an accident causing death, may be charged in the criminal court for manslaughter and he may also, for the same act, be sued in the civil court for negligence.

The category of a law is therefore not a function of the particular activity involved. The category of law is determined by the consequence of its breach.

Courts of Criminal Law

The court's process is initiated in a criminal matter by means of a document called either an indictment or an information (which may then be followed by committal proceedings and indictment). The process is called a prosecution. It is in most cases initiated by the state's representatives being either police officers, clerks of courts, or the Office of the Director of Public

Prosecutions (ODPP). The person who suffered the injury, resulting in a prosecution, is called the virtual complainant. That person may also initiate the process, which is then called a private prosecution.

Jamaica is a monarchy and therefore prosecutions are commenced in the name of the Crown. This is because the King or Queen (as the case may be) personifies the state. Where the monarch is a Queen cases are entitled *The Queen v (the name of the accused)*, where the monarch is a King cases are entitled *The King v (the name of the accused)*. In law reports the case will be entitled *R v (the name of the accused)*. The R stands for Regina or Rex, depending on whether it is a Queen or a King on the throne.

> *The R stands for Regina or Rex, depending on whether it is a Queen or a King on the throne.*

Most serious criminal cases, such as murder, rape, and burglary are tried by a judge and a jury.[1] A great many criminal cases are tried by a judge alone. The prosecutor is required to prove his case beyond a reasonable doubt or, in other words, so that the judge or jury is sure. The result in a criminal trial will be a verdict of either guilty or not guilty. In rare cases a jury will be unable to arrive at a verdict and in such cases a retrial is usually ordered.

Once convicted, the person accused of crime will become a convict and will then be sentenced. This may consist of a reprimand (called an admonition), a fine, imprisonment, or sentence of death. In certain circumstances the court can give a suspended sentence or can make community service orders against the convict. Sentencing is the responsibility of the judge and depends on the peculiar facts and circumstances of the case and of the convicted person.

Many crimes are created by statute law; however, there are also common law crimes. Conspiracy (an agreement either, to do an unlawful act or, to do a lawful act by unlawful means) is an example of a common law crime.

Courts of Civil Law

Civil laws largely govern relations between the *civilians* or citizens of Jamaica. These laws relate to almost every sphere of human activity from the personal (Family Law) to business (Corporate or Commercial Law).

The civil court's process is initiated either by a Claim Form or, by a Fixed Date Claim Form in the Supreme Court or by Plaint in the Parish Court. The process is called a lawsuit, a civil legal action, or a Claim. The person initiating is a Claimant, the person sued is the Defendant. A civil action bears the names of the parties to it, for example, *John Davis v Michael Barnes*. The government (or the state) can sue and be sued and, in such circumstances, the Attorney-General is the named party.[2]

> *The person initiating is a Claimant, the person sued is the Defendant.*

The Claimant in a civil lawsuit is required to prove his claim on a balance of probabilities. That is, it must be shown that it is more probable than not that something occurred in the way one alleges. At the end of a civil trial, the court gives a decision in the form of a judgment.

Most civil cases are tried by a judge alone.[3] The judge will deliver a judgment setting out his decision and the reasons for that decision. In the superior courts these judgments are recorded and put in law reports. The decision of the court may be to find the defendant liable or not liable. If liable, the court will usually award damages, which constitute monetary compensation. There are other civil remedies such as a declaration, an injunction, restitution, or specific performance. These are called private law remedies.

In the sphere of public law, where the claim is against a public official or the state for breach of constitutional or statutory duties, the major remedies are damages, a declaration, mandamus, prohibition, certiorari and habeas corpus. Habeas Corpus is an order to produce before the court someone held in custody so a judge can decide if that person's detention is lawful or unlawful. It is very important and serves to protect citizens from an abuse of state power. Certiorari is an order allowing a wrong decision to be quashed. Prohibition is, as its name suggests, an order preventing certain conduct, and Mandamus is an order directing that something be done. A Declaratory judgment states what the legal position is, and although binding, it is not enforceable without further legal action. Damages are awarded on the same basis as in private law cases and generally are compensatory.

> *Habeas Corpus is an order to produce before the court someone held in custody so a judge can decide if that person's detention is lawful or unlawful.*

There are many types of civil wrongs (called causes of action), some being creations of the common law, others are creations of statute and some are created by the Constitution. Claims which may be brought include claims for: breach of contract; quasi contract or other claims in equity; the torts (wrongs) of Negligence, Trespass (to person or property), Fraud, Defamation, Nuisance, or any of a number of others too numerous to mention; for Constitutional relief; for Divorce or other matrimonial relief; for breach of statutory duty; and, for Judicial Review. The categories of civil wrong are as many and varied as the categories of crime and are all too numerous to mention here.

Rules of Evidence

A trial in both the criminal and civil court serves the same basic purpose: to resolve an issue by a process giving a fair hearing to all parties involved. It was not always so. The process used to involve a joust or battle between the contenders. Then there used to be a process of compurgation (an acquittal from a charge or accusation obtained by the oaths of witnesses). This involved persons memorizing sworn statements, the winner being the one with more of such persons. There was a time when a person accused of a crime was not allowed to be present at his/her trial. Later, the accused was only allowed to observe his trial and so was not allowed to speak.

Today all trials in Jamaica are presided over by a judge whose role is that of an impartial adjudicator. He is to keep the scales evenly balanced between the parties. The prosecutor (or in a civil case the claimant) will give evidence first by calling such evidence as he deems necessary to prove his case. After the prosecution's case is closed, the defence will then present its case by giving evidence and calling witnesses. When all the evidence is in, each side will make submissions (referred to as an 'address' in the criminal court) to the judge or, to the judge and jury, as the case may be.

In a trial it is the nature and quality of evidence called which often determines the result. Evidence consists of the spoken word, documents, objects, scientific opinion, or observation. The general rule is that evidence must be relevant to the facts in issue meaning it must go to prove or disprove a relevant fact. The trial judge has the duty to determine whether evidence is admissible.

Evidence, even if relevant, will be omitted if it is inconsistent with certain exclusionary rules. The courts require that the best evidence be put forward unless an adequate explanation is proffered (the best evidence rule). This means, for example, one ought not to tender the copy of a document if the original is still in existence and available. Another exclusionary rule is the common law rule against hearsay evidence. There are many technical definitions of this rule however, simply put,

> *...'a person can only give evidence of what they saw, felt, smelt, tasted, did or heard themselves not what anyone else said or wrote.'*

it is that, 'a person can only give evidence of what they saw, felt, smelt, tasted, did or heard themselves not what anyone else said or wrote.'[4] A witness is allowed to give evidence of something said where the purpose of giving the evidence is to establish the fact that it was said and not the truth of what was said. If, for example, there is a motor vehicle accident and it is important in the trial to establish that someone was still alive in the car when firefighters arrived, evidence that firefighters heard a passenger say, 'my leg is broken,' may be admissible.

This rule of evidence explains why 'viral videos' are not always admissible in evidence. The authenticity has to be established usually by calling the maker of the video. It is not always possible to prove its origin notwithstanding how convincing the video may appear.

The hearsay rule was developed by Common Law judges in an attempt to admit only reliable evidence. However it proved to be too restrictive and virtually unworkable in its purest form.[5] The common law judges and statute therefore over time created several exceptions to the hearsay rule. The major exceptions to the hearsay rule are: public documents; evidence of things said in the course of the event in question (called *res gestae* evidence); a dying declaration where the person speaking knew he was about to die; computer-generated evidence; business documents created in the ordinary course of business; statements where the person who wrote or signed it is dead or cannot practicably be made available, and confessions or admissions made against interest. A confession will only be admitted into evidence if it is voluntary (that is not made due to fear or hope of advantage from a person in authority). The requirement that persons criminally charged be cautioned, is designed to reduce the chance of an involuntary confession.[6]

A judge has a discretion to exclude relevant, and otherwise admissible, evidence if its prejudicial effect outweighs its probative value. If, for instance, a photograph of the deceased at a crime scene is so gruesome that it may cause a jury to give a verdict based on anger, sympathy, or outrage, rather than anything of a probative nature in the photograph, the judge will rule it inadmissible. Evidence illegally obtained is admissible provided the circumstances make it just to admit such evidence.[7]

There are several other rules of evidence and lawyers spend many years studying them.

Evidence in Chief, Cross-Examination, and Re-examination

Witnesses are integral to the trial process. Their evidence *in chief* is the answers to questions put to them by the party who calls them to give evidence. In the civil court sometimes evidence in chief is by affidavit, at other times witnesses may give witness statements, which stand as their evidence in chief. In the criminal courts witnesses almost always give oral evidence.

In all trials, whether civil or criminal, the witness will be required to attend for cross-examination. Cross-examination is the process by which a witness's evidence in chief is tested. The lawyer for the other side is able to ask probing and searching questions of the witness. The cross-examiner may challenge the witness's observations and opportunity to make them. He may use documents or other real evidence such as photographs to challenge the witness's evidence. Cross-examination is integral to the trial process and occurs in both civil and criminal cases. The case against someone should be put to them in cross-examination so that they have an opportunity to respond to it.

After the witness is cross-examined the lawyer who called the witness is permitted to re-examine him. The process of re-examination allows for clarification of any ambiguous matters, or a response to anything new which may have emerged during cross-examination.

Whenever witnesses give oral evidence (whether in chief, cross-examination or re-examination) they are required to take an oath. A witness is allowed to swear the oath to the deity of his choice.[8] Witnesses who have a conscientious objection to taking an oath are allowed to affirm. This applies whether the witness is giving evidence in the criminal or the civil court.

Evidence is sometimes taken from remote locations with the aid of video conferencing and other technology. This existed before but proved particularly useful during the time of the COVID-19 pandemic. It allows witnesses under real threat or who cannot practicably attend in person to give evidence from another location.

Expert or Forensic Evidence

Some witnesses are allowed to give, as evidence, their opinion on matters that are relevant to the facts in issue. Witnesses who give opinions, based upon their study or experience in a particular science or area of activity, are called expert witnesses. An expert witness must satisfy the court of both his expertise and the soundness of his opinion.

In the criminal court, experts usually give oral evidence. In the civil courts, on the other hand, experts often provide written reports. These must be in the format required by the rules of court.[9] In both courts experts may be cross-examined by opposing counsel. An expert may be tested on his conclusions, scientific methods, training, expertise, competence, integrity, and observations.

The expert's first duty is to the court. He has a duty to speak the truth and give his honest opinion. The expert will, if he asks to do so, be allowed to refresh his or her memory from any notes he made at the time he did the experiments or made observations. Experts may also rely on the published opinions or research of other experts to support their opinion.

An expert cannot be compelled to give an opinion. However, once the opinion has been given he may, as with any other witness, be compelled by witness summons or subpoena to give evidence about it. An expert who knowingly lies to the court may, like any other witness, be charged with perjury.

There are several types of expert evidence, including Medical, Psychological, Handwriting, Blood Typing, Fingerprinting, DNA, Accounting, Land Valuation, Market Research, and even Dog Handling. The categories of expert evidence are not closed and new sciences when developed may be admitted in evidence to help prove facts in issue in any given case.

Public Right to Attend Court

The court is a public place,[10] and all citizens have a right to enter and observe any trial, civil or criminal. This is subject only to space constraints and the few categories of cases that are by law, rules of court, or the trial judge's ruling, to be heard in camera. An in camera trial is one held in private usually for the protection of victims and witnesses. Public accessibility to trials may be improved by allowing the live broadcast of proceedings, but this may create risks to persons giving evidence. However, Jamaican courts have a media policy which outlines the circumstances in which live and other reporting may be done.[11]

Persons who attend court to give evidence as witnesses are not allowed to be present in court during the trial before they give their evidence. This is to prevent the intended witness from hearing the evidence of earlier witnesses. After giving evidence, witnesses are allowed to remain in court. The expert witness does not, unless the judge says otherwise, have to remain outside of court before he gives his evidence. Parties to a claim, as well as accused persons, are entitled to be present in court for the duration of the trial.

Result of Trial

After all the evidence is in, counsel for each side will address the court. The court will thereafter give a decision based upon its assessment of the evidence presented. The jury (or judge) in a criminal trial gives a verdict and, the judge in a civil case, will deliver a judgment.

Contempt of Court

A judge has the power to protect the court's process, and the integrity of that process, in a summary way. This means that any person who adversely affects proceedings in court by words, acts, or omissions may be punished for contempt of court.[12] The judge may immediately order the incarceration of someone whose disruptive behaviour is sustained and such as to prevent the trial proceeding.

Criticism of the court or judge however harsh is not by itself sufficient to constitute a contempt of court. This is because, as Lord Atkin said, justice is not a '*cloistered virtue*.'[13] In this regard, there is a distinction to be drawn between conduct in the face of the court impacting proceedings and conduct more remote which does not.

Before punishing a person for contempt the trial judge should give that person a fair hearing. He does this by asking the person to show cause why he ought not to be punished for contempt.[14]

Alternative Methods of Dispute Resolution

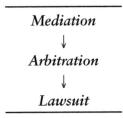

Mediation

↓

Arbitration

↓

Lawsuit

The trial process is one way of resolving disputes, but there are others. Some civil disputes are resolved by way of a process called arbitration. This allows the parties to a dispute to agree on the adjudicator, to control the costs of and time line for adjudication, and to have their dispute resolved in private. Arbitration only occurs with the agreement of both parties. Jamaica has a modern Arbitration Act.

Another form of dispute resolution is mediation. This is a structured negotiation in which a trained person facilitates discussions between the parties. Mediation is now a compulsory part of the civil procedure in Jamaica's courts. Mediation is also used in the preliminary stage of some criminal law issues usually those involving domestic conflicts.

Conclusion

This then is how our courts function. Citizens are encouraged to take the time to attend court and observe justice in action.

8.
Other Institutions of Governance

We have looked at the Constitution of Jamaica and the institutions it created. There are however other institutions, in our society, that perform equally important roles. Some are created by legislation and others by citizens of Jamaica in their private capacity. They may take the form of statutory corporations, commissions of Parliament, private companies, or private member organizations.

In this chapter we will examine some of these institutions in no particular order.

Trade Unions

A trade union is an organization, usually of workers, concerned with relations between employers and workers. It is dedicated to the advancement of the interest of its members. This is primarily by way of negotiating for improved wages and working conditions.

The trade union was not always an accepted institution. In the late nineteenth and early twentieth century, any combination of workers, which had the object of organizing strikes, was regarded as illegal. This is because an employee's refusal to work is a breach of a contract of employment. Therefore, an agreement to jointly breach the contract constituted, at common law, an unlawful combination. The organizations were also thought to be in restraint of trade. The conditions under which workers were employed were such that they had to come together to organize and fight for improvements. This occurred in many places in the world.

Eventually trade unions were recognized as legitimate organizations with which employers could negotiate. In Jamaica a Trade Union Act was passed in 1919. This statute legalized the formation of trade unions although it did not make legal the act of breaking ones contract of employment. In 1975 the Labour Relations and Industrial Disputes Act was passed into law. This statute established a legal framework for the resolution of industrial (work-related) disputes between employer and employee. It established an Industrial Disputes Tribunal, which unlike a court, has statutory power to order the reinstatement of employees who were wrongfully dismissed.

The Jamaica Constabulary Force

The police force, as this organization is more commonly known, was established in 1866 as a direct result of the Morant Bay Rebellion. In 1935, with the passage of the Constabulary Force Act of that year, it was reorganized. Its purpose was in part to prevent unrest in the colony, and this may explain why section 3 of the Act says the Jamaica Constabulary Force 'shall be partially under Military Organisation and Discipline.'[1] The expressly stated duty of the police pursuant to section 13 is:

> ...to keep watch by day and by night, to preserve the peace, to detect crime, apprehend or summon before a justice persons found committing any offence or whom they may reasonably suspect of having committed any offence, or who may be charged with having committed any offence, to serve and to execute all summonses, warrants, subpoenas,

notices and criminal processes issued from any Court of Criminal Justice or by any justice in a criminal matter and to do and perform all the duties appertaining to the office of a Constable....

A police officer, as with any ordinary citizen, can arrest a person who commits a crime. He may, however, unlike the ordinary citizen, also effect arrest on reasonable suspicion that a crime has been, is being or, is about to be committed.[2] The police officer, unlike the ordinary citizen, is protected from legal action being taken against him if he did not act maliciously or without reasonable or probable cause.[3]

The Constabulary Force Act also details special powers of the police to create cordons and enforce curfews. It also provides for police pensions, gratuities, and disability allowances.

The General Legal Council and The Legal Education Authority

In 1972 the Legal Profession Act was passed. This statute made provision for legal training and the regulation of lawyers in Jamaica. By this statute, Parliament created one fused profession known as attorneys-at-law. Prior to this the profession had been divided into solicitors and barristers. Solicitors were unable to argue cases in the higher courts and worked mainly in their offices. They were responsible for collecting fees and taking instructions from the client before retaining the barrister who then argued the case in the higher court. The systems for regulation and discipline of barristers and solicitors were separate. This division in the profession, which still exists in England today,[4] was part of the English law brought to Jamaica.

Since the passage of the Legal Profession Act all attorneys-at-law can appear in any court and all are regulated by the

General Legal Council. That institution makes the rules governing the conduct of all attorneys-at-law practising in Jamaica. It initiates proceedings against attorneys-at-law who are alleged to have broken any of those rules. Enforcement of the rules, and hence the punishment of attorneys found guilty of infringement, is the responsibility of the Disciplinary Committee of the General Legal Council. Any person who is aggrieved by an act of professional misconduct, committed by an attorney-at-law, may report the matter to the Disciplinary Committee. Many attorneys-at-law have had to be disciplined over the years. This is necessary if the public is to be assured of competent and honest professional representation. The reports of such proceedings can be viewed on the website of the General Legal Council.

The Legal Profession Act also created a Legal Education Authority which regulates the training and qualification to become an attorney-at-law. Legal Education is provided in cooperation with other countries in the Caribbean who are party to a treaty establishing the regional law schools. At present, anyone wishing to qualify as an attorney-at-law should first obtain a law degree and then attend a regional law school.[5] Upon the successful completion of examinations, a Legal Education Certificate will be issued. The candidate must then apply to the court to be admitted to practise law. A judge of the Supreme Court, after hearing the application and upon being satisfied of the candidate's good character and academic qualifications, will make an order admitting him or her to the practice of law. The applicant is then said to be *called* to the Bar.[6]

All attorneys-at-law are officers of the court. The judge therefore also has the power to implement disciplinary measures, in a summary way, over attorneys-at-law.[7] This power is rarely exercised in modern times. Judges more often than not refer attorneys who they believe have misconducted themselves in a professional respect to the General Legal Council.

Jamaica continues to maintain another type of divide in the legal profession which came with colonialism. This is the division between ordinary counsel and Queen's Counsel (QC). The latter receive that designation on the basis of excellence at the Bar or because they hold certain public offices. The Prime Minister confers the title having received advice from a broad-based committee of lawyers, judges, and Queen's Counsel.

Corporations and Unincorporated Associations

Within modern society individuals get together in groups to organize and attain an objective. It may be for the purpose of sports, such as to form a football team or club. It may be for community protection, such as a neighbourhood watch. It may also be economic, such as to pool resources to start a business venture or cooperative society. The objectives will largely determine the legal structure chosen to represent the group.

One basic structure is called an Unincorporated Association. Here the individuals will draft and sign an agreement, usually called a constitution, to detail how the association will operate. Any person who wishes to become a member will sign an application form and agree to be bound by the constitution of the association. The Unincorporated Association is usually governed by an elected executive. The executive and all members are personally responsible and therefore liable for any acts or omissions done in the name of the association.

The Trading Partnership is another form of grouping. In this instance individuals come together to conduct business under a trade or business name. This is regulated by the Registration of Business Names Act. Partnerships are also the means by which professionals group together to offer their services. In this arrangement the individual members remain liable for the acts of the partnership, as well as the acts of each partner on behalf of the partnership. Partnerships may involve any number of persons, and its rules are governed by the agreement entered into, between and among the partners.

The Corporation is the third main form of organization. It is sometimes called a company and is usually formed for the purpose of doing business, but there are corporations formed for charitable and other reasons such as to *hold* property. The Companies Act of Jamaica determines how corporate institutions are created and regulated. The corporation is a separate legal entity from its members and can sue or be sued in its own name. In other words it is a legal person and can enter contracts and conduct business in its name. The members of the company are shareholders who will, in accordance with its rules or articles of association, elect or appoint a board of directors.

The company acts through its board of directors. Save for statutory exceptions, usually having to do with taxation, neither the members nor the directors are personally liable for any acts or omissions of the company. That is why when doing business with a company, particularly where the company may owe you money, it is wise to obtain a personal guarantee from its directors or shareholders.

Corporations are of different types, and may be private or public. The number of members in a private company is limited whereas there is no limit to the shareholders in a public company. The major difference between the two is that the shares of a private company cannot be sold without first being offered to other members of the company. In a public company on the other hand the members may sell their shares at any time to anyone. The Jamaica Stock Exchange lists public companies for this reason, and it is the place where trading in shares occurs.[8]

The corporation, whether public or private, uses the issuing of shares as a means of raising capital. Prospective shareholders must put money into the company in order to acquire shares. Once acquired, however, the shares become the property of the shareholder and can therefore, in the case of the public company, be traded on the Stock Exchange. When companies need to raise capital, new or bonus shares will be issued. Shares also determine how much of the company's profits a shareholder receives, this is called a dividend.

Some companies are limited not by shares but by guarantee. These are usually trusts or charitable corporations created for a specific purpose. These companies do not issue shares but instead have members who subscribe. Unlike public and private companies, they do not pay dividends.

The Companies Act contains a great number of rules concerning the duties of directors, the winding up of companies and other matters. It is always best to obtain the advice of an attorney-at-law when dealing with corporate matters.

Registrar of Companies

This office is established by section 351 of the Companies Act. It is a registry for all companies doing business in Jamaica, whether incorporated within Jamaica or not. The duties of the Registrar of Companies are wide and varied. Certified copies of documents filed with the Registrar are admissible in court as evidence without a need to produce an original.

Registrar of Births and Deaths

This office, also called the Registrar General's Department, was established by the Registration (Births and Deaths) Act, which was passed in 1881. The statute has been amended many times. Its purpose is to ensure that all children born in Jamaica are registered and a record kept of all persons who die here. The Act places the responsibility on the father or mother of the child to register the birth. The occupier of any home in which a child is born is also obliged to register the birth. The Act regulates the issuing of birth (and death) certificates and the correlation, if necessary, of such events. The public has a right to access and obtain copies of the records. The Marriage Act by section 42 makes the Registrar General of Births and Deaths the Registrar General of Marriages. Section 28 allows marriages to be carried out by a civil Registrar and without the need for a religious ceremony. Marriage officers are also appointed under that Act which states that persons under 18 years of age require the consent of their parent or legal guardian to get married.

Registrar of Titles

All land in Jamaica vests in the Jamaican state, which is personified by the Crown. Since colonial times the state has granted or sold land to various persons. Such persons are said to have received a legal estate. Owners of land therefore have what is called a *fee simple* estate or interest in the land. More than one person may hold a fee simple interest in the same parcel of land. If so they hold either as joint tenants or as tenants in common. The practical difference between the two is that upon the death of one joint tenant (owner) his entire interest goes to the other surviving joint owner. Tenants in common, however, always have a separate interest so that after death their interest in the land goes to their estate. A tenant in common can therefore sell or gift by will his interest without the consent of the other co-owners.

A landowner (the holder of an estate in fee simple) may sell his land to others. He may also rent, sometimes called a lease, the land to others who become his tenants. The owner of land may also grant permission to someone to occupy land without the creation of any legal interest. This is called a licence. The difference between a lease and a licence is that the tenant (lessee) has exclusive possession of the land. The tenant is also entitled to the protections available under the Rent Restriction Act.[9] A licensee on the other hand does not have exclusive possession and may be asked to leave at any time. A contractual licensee may enjoy certain rights and have responsibilities determined by the terms of his licence.

Anyone in possession of land who is not a fee simple owner, a tenant or a licensee, is a trespasser. In Jamaica, trespass to land was made a crime by statute.[10] Another word for trespasser is squatter. Someone who occupies another person's land and treats the land as his own to the exclusion of all others, for a specified period of time will be entitled to apply for legal ownership. This is because the Limitations of Actions Act bars a claim for repossession by the true owner after that period of time.[11]

In 1889 the Registration of Titles Act was passed. Its purpose was to put in place a regime for the registration and titling of land in Jamaica. Prior to this enactment all land in the island was held by common law title. This meant persons had to demonstrate a good root of title by producing receipts or other documentation showing purchase, devolution, or gift. This could prove very difficult after generations had passed. It was also an inexact system and often led to controversy and boundary disputes. The state therefore created a regime for the registration of land, and the issue of a title, which could not be disputed, save and except by proof of fraud. The system of titling implemented is known as the Torrens System. It was popularized in Australia.

Under the Torrens system the Registrar of Titles has a duty to check and verify documents submitted and thereafter issue a title to the holder or holders of the fee simple (that is the owner). The owner can sell that title by means of a transfer, which, once executed, confers ownership to someone else. Intended purchasers of land therefore need look no further than the title in order to verify who owns it. However, all persons intending to buy land should visit the land and have a surveyor confirm that the title relates to the land shown, that the boundaries are intact, and to ensure there are no trespassers in possession. They should also have the title scrutinized by an attorney-at-law to ensure there are no caveats or other registered interests on the title.

The distinction between joint owners who are tenants in common and those who are joint tenants continued to exist after the passage of the Registration of Titles Act. The Titles Office is now a part of the National Land Agency from which the Registrar of Titles operates.

Office of the Ombudsman and Public Defender

The Public Defenders Act establishes the Office of Ombudsman and Public Defender. Both roles are performed by the same individual. The Ombudsman accepts and investigates complaints by members of the public against state bodies or ministries, reports to Parliament and recommends compensation or other means of resolving the complaint. The Public Defender investigates, makes recommendations, and also funds legal action, where a breach of a constitutional right is involved. These services are provided without charge to the public.

Political Ombudsman

The office of political ombudsman is established by the Political Ombudsman (Interim) Act. It is a commission of Parliament meaning that the holder of the office reports to the Parliament of Jamaica. Its function is to investigate the conduct of political parties in Jamaica with specific reference to the breach of any agreed codes of conduct or any action which may prejudice good relations between political parties. The Political Ombudsman is appointed by the Governor-General, after consultation with both the Prime Minister and the Leader of the Opposition, for a term of seven years. The statute is *interim* because it is Parliament's intent to insert the position in the Constitution of Jamaica.

Contractor General/Integrity Commission and the Committee for the Prevention of Corruption

A Commission for the Prevention of Corruption was established by the Corruption Prevention Act. Its functions are to obtain and examine statutory declarations as to income from all public servants, make independent enquiries and investigations into such declarations as may be necessary, investigate complaints relating to acts of corruption, and conduct on its own initiative investigation into acts of corruption.

The Act provides a broad and comprehensive definition of what may constitute an act of corruption. These, for example, include the acceptance of a gift whether directly or indirectly for doing or omitting to do any act in the performance of public duties. Both the giver and receiver of the gift are liable to be prosecuted for the crime of corruption. The detailed provision as to what constitutes an act of corruption is contained in section 14 of the Act and should be read by every public servant. It is the duty of the Commission for the Prevention of Corruption to report any acts of corruption to the relevant services commission and to the Office of the Director of Public Prosecutions or the Director of Corruption Prosecutions.

In 2015, Parliament passed the Integrity Commission Act. This statute created the Integrity Commission whose function is to (a) promote propriety and integrity among persons exercising public functions, (b) strengthen measures for prevention and detection of corruption and prosecution of corruption, (c) ensure government contracts are awarded fairly and in a financially prudent manner, and (d) enhance public confidence that acts of corruption will be appropriately dealt with. The commission is a commission of Parliament and a body corporate which means it may sue or be sued in its own name. It is empowered to prosecute acts of corruption and for this purpose the statute creates the post of *Director of Corruption Prosecution*.

Although the Corruption Prevention Act has not been repealed the Integrity Commission is now responsible for many of the things hitherto done by the Commission for the Prevention of Corruption.

Independent Commission of Investigations

The Independent Commission of Investigations (INDECOM) is a commission of Parliament created by a statute of the same name. Its purpose is to conduct investigations into alleged misconduct by the security forces. The commission has wide powers of access to documents and other material and can summon witnesses and control the scene of any incidents. After some uncertainty the courts have determined that INDECOM does not have the power to prosecute and that this is reserved for the Director of Public Prosecutions.[12] INDECOM, therefore, is to make reports and recommendations.

Consumer Affairs Commission

This institution is established by the Consumer Protection Act. Its purpose is to investigate and report on consumer complaints regarding the sale of goods and the provision of services. The commission may also investigate issues related to the availability of goods or services. It has the power to institute legal proceedings on behalf of the consumer and will also endeavour to resolve disagreements. The Consumer Protection Act, as the name implies, has important safeguards as it relates to the conduct of persons offering goods or services for sale. The commission serves to ensure these duties are not breached or if breached that the consumer has an easily accessible remedy.

Firearm Licensing Authority

The Firearms Act establishes the Firearm Licensing Authority (FLA). The Authority is responsible for the granting, renewal and revocation of licences to use, import and/or sell firearms in Jamaica. There are several different types of permits and licences connected with the use and ownership of firearms, and the FLA oversees them all.

The Firearms Act also creates several offences relative to the use and possession of firearms and ammunition. It is an offence under the Act to lose a firearm due to negligence.

Rent Board

This institution is created by the Rent Restriction Act. That is a law which regulates the relationship between landlords and tenants. The Act restricts the circumstances in which a landlord may recover possession of premises from a tenant and also controls the rent landlords may charge.

The Rent Board can hear and determine certain issues between a landlord and his tenant. It may also exempt certain premises from the operation of the Act.

Transport Authority and the Island Traffic Authority

The Road Traffic Act was passed in 1938 and has been amended on several occasions over the years. Its purpose is to regulate the operation of vehicular traffic on Jamaica's roads. The statute creates motor vehicle offences and establishes standards for the vehicles on the roads.

The Act creates Traffic Authorities whose responsibility it is to regulate and control traffic, inspect motor vehicles, test applicants for driver's licences, keep records, and enforce offences under the Act among other things.

The Transport Authority is created by the Transport Authority Act. Its purpose is to monitor and regulate the use of public passenger vehicles on Jamaica's roads.

The Adoption Board

This agency is established by the Children (Adoption of) Act. Its purpose is to make arrangements for the adoption of children and to investigate and report on such arrangements. Adoption can occur not only in respect of children who have no parents but can be initiated by parents who wish to voluntarily surrender their children for adoption. The Board exists to ensure, as far as is humanly possible, that the best interest of the child is secured. No adoption should occur without an application to the Board. Although it is common practice for Jamaican families to take in other children, complete legal authority for a child is only possible by way of adoption under the Act and/or by order of the court. The guardianship of children (sometimes referred to as foster parenting) is regulated by the Children (Guardianship and Custody) Act.[13]

Children's Advocate

The Office of the Children's Advocate is a Commission of Parliament established under the Child Care and Protection Act. The purpose of the Act is to promote the best interest, safety, and well-being of Jamaica's children. The Children's Advocate is appointed by the Governor-General after consultation with the Prime Minister and the Leader of the Opposition and is empowered to protect and enforce the rights of children. The Children's Advocate may also represent any child brought before the court, whether criminal or civil. The Child Care and Protection Act has far reaching provisions relating to the welfare of children generally as well as for children in places of safety and children's homes.

Office of Utilities Regulation (OUR)

This institution was created to license and regulate the operation of public utilities in Jamaica. It is created by the Office of Utilities Regulation Act. Members of the public who have complaints in relation to the provision of light, water, telecommunication, and other services may make them to the OUR.

Electoral Commission

The electoral commission is created by the Electoral Commission (Interim) Act which was passed in 2006. Its stated purpose is to safeguard the democratic foundation of Jamaica by enabling eligible voters to elect by free and fair elections their representatives to govern Jamaica. It represents the joint effort of Jamaica's major political parties and is the successor to previous institutions established since 1962.

Its role and function is crucial for the maintenance of confidence in Jamaican election results.

Jamaica Defence Force

The Defence Act was passed on July 31, 1962. It established the Jamaica Defence Force whose purpose is to defend Jamaica and maintain order and such other duties as may from time to time be assigned. This in recent times has included emergency relief in Jamaica and the wider Caribbean as well as assistance to the police in crime fighting.

The Act creates a body known as the Defence Board, responsible for command, discipline, and administration of the Defence Force.

The Act contains detailed provisions for the recruitment, remuneration, and discipline of the members of the military.

The Government Trustee and The Supervisor of Insolvency

It sometimes happens that persons and companies are unable, or fail, to pay their debts 'as they generally become due'. It used to be that such individuals might be placed in bankruptcy and companies wound up. In 2014, the Insolvency Act was passed offering a further alternative. A person (individual or corporate) in such difficulty is now allowed, in certain circumstances, to be rehabilitated to a solvent position. The process requires the cooperation of creditors (the persons to whom the money is owed) and involves a licensed trustee. The process is commenced by lodging either a 'Proposal' or a 'Notice of Intention to make a Proposal' with the Supervisor of Insolvency. This will automatically, but temporarily, stay all proceedings by creditors to recover their debts. The Act creates the position of 'Government Trustee' and 'Supervisor of Insolvency'. These officers see to the due execution of insolvency proceedings.

9.
Rights and the Rule of Law in Jamaican Society

In order to truly appreciate the importance of constitutional rights it is necessary to say a little about their origin. This is because the rights stated in the Constitution (as to which see chapter 6) were neither gifted to Jamaicans by anyone nor, 'natural,' to man.[1]

The Origin of Rights

Human rights may be more accurately regarded as a product of society's social, political, and economic progress. Think about it, when humans, such as the Taínos, lived in groups of hunter gatherers, life was brutish and short. Social misfits were stoned to death or expelled from the tribe. There was no concept of a guaranteed human or individual right because the survival of the tribe was the most important consideration. At a later stage of human development, in particular in Europe, a feudal or peasant farming society evolved. The need for order and obedience to the King or Noble was then paramount. There was not much scope or concern for individualism. Similarly, the slave society created in Jamaica did not recognize human rights for the vast majority living in that society.

Mercantilism, and the industrialization following, changed the social dynamics of feudal society in Europe. Labour became socialized as hundreds toiled in factories which were located in population centres called cities. Trade and great surpluses resulted in increased wealth for the industrialist and the mercantilist. These *nouveaux riche* eventually found common cause with the working classes and leveraged for a greater say in the conduct of public affairs. There was eventually a challenge to the authoritarian rule of the monarch and the landed or propertied persons. This process although occurring at a different pace in different societies, often resulted in the empowerment of the individual and a recognition of rights.

In England a King was executed as early as 1649 resulting in a republican state for 11 years. In 1660, a royalist-minded Parliament voted to restore the monarchy, but the new king (James II) chose to dissolve Parliament and rule by edict. This act, as well as his Roman Catholic sympathies, led to revolt and a transfer of support to his daughter Mary and her protestant husband William of Orange (a Dutchman). The resultant 'Glorious' (but relatively peaceful) Revolution heralded the primacy of Parliament, a Bill of Rights Act of 1689 and the Act of Settlement of 1701. These events marked the commencement of the English constitutional structure as we know it today.[2] The English revolutionary process ended in compromise as political power was transferred to a people's parliament[3] even as the hereditary monarch was restored.

In 1776, American colonists declared *no taxation without representation*. Their revolution resulted in a written Constitution, which rejected the monarchy, gave power to the people and, created a separation of powers in the new system of government. In 1789, a Bill of Rights was introduced to the American Constitution. That was also the year the French revolution began, in the course of which, the King Louis XIV eventually and literally lost his head. The French people declared *'liberté, égalité, fraternité'* (liberty, equality, brotherhood).[4]

Throughout history therefore the recognition of human rights occurred after a process of economic, social, and political struggle for change. This is also true of the right to freedom for the enslaved Africans in the New World. The rights proclaimed in Magna Carta and the American Constitution did not automatically extend to them. The United States, that bastion of liberty, did not abolish the institution of slavery until 1865 with the thirteenth amendment to their Constitution.[5] The French revolutionaries declared slavery abolished in 1794, but Napoleon Bonaparte revoked that pronouncement. France finally abolished slavery in 1848.[6] The English had already done so in 1834. This, as we saw in earlier chapters, occurred only after Jamaicans and others fought many wars of rebellion.

Law in Jamaica Today

In 1962, when Jamaica's Constitution was drafted, the rights declared by the United Nations had already been concretized in other parts of the Commonwealth. It is therefore no surprise that a Bill of Rights was inserted.[7] The Fundamental Rights and Freedoms as stated in the *new* Bill of Rights (as amended in 2011) are admirable. The rights are subject only to (a) the sections of the Constitution which give Parliament the power, with the requisite majority, to suspend or amend the rights, (b) curtailment as is '*demonstrably justified in a free and democratic society*'[8] and, (c) the rights and freedoms of others.

Jamaica is a modern society in which the institutions of government function alongside private enterprise. The labour, capital, ingenuity and technical knowledge of Jamaicans produce goods and services. Some of these goods and services are bought and sold here in Jamaica. However, much of it is exported and in that way Jamaica (and Jamaicans) earn foreign exchange. The foreign exchange (currency) is necessary so that Jamaica can purchase oil for energy and a range of other products we do not produce for ourselves. All this economic activity takes place in the context of laws regulating behaviour and the boundaries which all are expected to understand and respect. Where there is deviation, that is a breach of the law, then there is recourse to the courts.

The law, as established in the Constitution of Jamaica, is premised on individual freedom. This means that unless something is prohibited by law, then a person is free to do it. Constitutional rights are guaranteed and are not to be reduced except in any of the circumstances outlined above. That is the reason, for example, that Jamaicans are free to move about unless there is reasonable cause to suspect that a crime has been, is being, or is about to be committed, or unless there is some reason having to do with public safety or road traffic control, to curtail that freedom.[9]

Function of Law in Society[10]

The two categories of the law are, as we have seen in chapter 7, the criminal and the civil. Criminal offences are usually creations of a statute. When a criminal law is breached the state is often the enforcing entity. Conduct prohibited by the criminal law is called crime. For example, the Larceny Act deals with stealing and related crimes. The Offences Against the Person Act prohibits rape, murder, and other offences like those. The Road Traffic Act details a multitude of offences related to the use of the road. In more modern times, statutes such as the Proceeds of Crime Act (POCA) make it an offence to knowingly accept money or property earned by virtue of criminal conduct. It is impossible to list here all the conduct made criminal by law. Therefore, it is prudent before embarking on a new venture or enterprise to have a lawyer check whether it is prohibited by law. This is because many activities by law require permission, in the form of a licence, from a relevant state agency. The sale of alcohol, for example, can only be done legally from licensed premises. Operating without the required licence usually attracts sanctions under the criminal law.

Civil Law is no less important than criminal law. The peace and good governance of society demands that both categories of law are enforced. Civil Law governs relations between individuals. Where businesspeople enter into a contract if one acts in breach of that contract the aggrieved (innocent) party may seek to have the contract enforced by legal action in the civil courts. A contract is an agreement for consideration, that is, in which value is exchanged, and to which the parties intended legal consequences to attach. A contract may be oral or in writing but when in writing it makes proof of the terms of the contract, that much easier.

A very old law, the Statute of Frauds,[11] states that contracts involving land must be *evidenced* in writing. This means that some document referring to the land such as a receipt has to be in existence. Equity[12] by virtue of the principle of estoppel has ameliorated this very strict rule. If there has been part performance, by for example, the purchaser being put in possession, the other party may not be able to rely on the absence of evidence in writing to avoid his contractual duties. The Law of Contract is only one of a vast array of civil laws regulating behaviour.

The Law of *Torts*, a Latin word for wrongs, is a category of civil law which provides remedies for injury suffered under many and varied circumstances. If someone deliberately hits or attacks another person, not only is he guilty of the crime of assault and battery, but he may be sued in the civil court for trespass to that person. This applies also if a person injures another deliberately or recklessly, that is, not caring whether the other is affected. Negligence is another Tort. The law requires that persons take reasonable care whenever their actions, or omission to act, can reasonably be expected to affect another. The situations in which such a duty of care emerges are innumerable and range from the driving of an automobile to the production of items for consumption.

Family relations are also governed by the civil law and regulates how to get married or divorced. The duties of maintenance for children and spouse and how property is divided after a divorce are set out in statute law. Judicial decisions have explained and applied these laws.

The civil law also regulates specific types of contract. So, for example, the Rent Restriction Act, which creates some criminal offences, also establishes a Rent Board to resolve issues that may arise between a landlord and his tenant. Landlords may in certain instances apply for and obtain an exemption from the Rent Restriction Act. Intended tenants, particularly commercial tenants, should always enquire whether the premises are exempt prior to renting. An exemption means that the tenant will not be eligible for many of the protections provided under the Rent Restriction Act.

Role of the Attorney-at-law

Before engaging in a new business venture it is best, in today's complex world, to obtain the advice of an attorney-at-law who will provide professional guidance as to the applicable law and how to conduct business legally. Also, if you run afoul of the law, the attorney will represent you in court to the best of his or her ability.

Jamaica trains and certifies its own attorneys-at-law.[13] This was not always the case. Prior to the passage of the Legal Education Act, which created the Norman Manley Law

School, many lawyers were trained in England. They were called barristers and had the right to represent persons in the superior courts of record. Other lawyers, known as solicitors, also sat overseas examinations and had to be *articled* to a local firm of lawyers. The Legal Profession Act changed all that. All persons who wish to become lawyers must first obtain a law degree and then matriculate to a regional law school.[14] After graduation from law school, provided they are of good character, the person will be called to the bar and be known as an attorney-at-law. The *call to the bar* takes place in a superior court of record and is presided over by a puisne judge. The attorney-at-law in this way becomes an officer of the court. Attorneys-at-law are regulated by the General Legal Council (GLC), which has rules of conduct to protect clients and the profession. If they break any of these rules attorneys-at-law may be tried by the Disciplinary Committee of the GLC.

Jamaica today, therefore, has a developed legal system. We have courts of justice administered by an independent judiciary. The country has many lawyers and law firms willing and able to provide legal advice and representation to all who need it. There are legal aid clinics providing low cost services to assist those who cannot otherwise afford it. The state provides a publicly funded system of legal aid in criminal matters, whereby attorneys in private practice are paid by the state to represent the accused. There is a Public Defender who is also an Ombudsman. This office was designed specifically to safeguard the constitutional rights of Jamaica's citizens. In addition, Jamaica has an Independent Commissioner whose duty it is to investigate allegations of breach of duty by the country's security forces.

Rule of Law

The Rule of Law is a phrase you will hear from time to time. Another is Due Process of law. They both approximate to the same concept. It is the idea that in order to have a just society the law must apply equally to everyone both the governed and the governor. No one is above the law. If this is so then the lawmaker will be careful to make laws that are fair. Also, the law enforcer will do so in accordance with law. In order for the Rule of Law to exist there must be an independent and impartial body to administer the law. This in Jamaica is the Judiciary. The Constitution seeks to ensure an independent judiciary by giving judges security of tenure and preventing salary roll back, reduction of pension, and the abolition of the post of Judge whilst there is an office holder.[15]

Conclusion

Human rights as they exist today are the result of hundreds of years of societal development and social struggle. In Jamaica, the law (criminal and civil), the Constitution, the access to legal representation, and the existence of an independent and impartial judiciary all ensure that the rule of law prevails, that no one is above the law, and that justice is accessible to all who seek it. This is necessary for social stability, democracy, and economic activity to thrive.

10.
International Law, Law Enforcement, and The Caribbean Court of Justice

Jamaica is a state. Other words used are country or nation. So far in this book we have only been considering Jamaica's national law, that is, the law within Jamaica binding persons in Jamaica. In this chapter we will consider the law binding states.

International law, which is also referred to as the Law of Nations, is the law regulating relations between states.[1] International law establishes territorial and sea boundaries, international trade, when and how war is to be waged, and has rules related to shipping, air travel, and many other things.

The Making of International Law

The history of mankind has been one characterized by conflict. As tribes, societies, and nations grew they came into contact with each other. Sometimes there would be trade but other times there would be war. Nations made war with one another in order to expand territory, to control trade routes and, to capture colonies. In Europe there were many wars between and among the Dutch, the English, the Spanish, the French, and the Portuguese. The merchants of these nations really wanted to trade for profit, but constant war was expensive and interfered with trade.

War was counterproductive to commerce and the mercantilists preferred peace to war. Language and cultural differences had to be overcome, but in time binding rules were agreed upon between these mostly European states, thereby reducing sources of conflict. This was accomplished by agreeing to rules regulating where and how ships could be boarded, rights of passage, territorial seas, trade routes and prevention of piracy, among many other things. These rules often took the form of agreements, also called treaties or conventions.

The genesis of International Law, the Law of Nations, was therefore, the need for countries to avoid going to war and to ensure that, if war occurred, a certain standard of conduct was maintained.[2] So, for example, customary international law, the Hague Conventions of 1899 and 1907 and the Geneva Conventions of 1949 regulate the treatment of prisoners of war.

Disputes between states are usually resolved in one or more of the following ways:

- International arbitration (there is an International Court of Justice (ICJ)).
- International condemnation.
- Trade sanctions or embargoes.
- War or the Use of Force.

The international legal landscape was significantly impacted by two major twentieth century international conflicts. After the war of 1914–1918 (often called the Great War or the First World War), the League of Nations was formed. This international organization, designed to end all wars, failed to do so mainly because it had no teeth and was not fully supported by the then emerging power of the United States. In 1939 another war started in Europe and by 1941 had spread to include countries in the Pacific, northern Africa, and the United States. This Second World War ended in 1945. The German dictator Adolph Hitler led Germany to war by wrongfully invading other countries and breaking treaties. He also passed laws, within his country, which led to the execution of approximately six million innocent people because they were Jewish.[3] This state-sponsored persecution is known as the Holocaust.

After that war another attempt was therefore made by the victorious states to prevent a recurrence. They did three things:

1. Formed the United Nations (UN), which has a Security Council with power to approve military action in order to enforce International Law. In order for a decision to be taken, the five permanent member countries of the security council must be in agreement.[4]

2. Put on trial before an international tribunal, the leaders and others in Germany who were responsible for the atrocities. They were charged with *crimes against humanity,* tried, and those convicted were sentenced to death or imprisonment. Known as the *Nuremberg* Trials as most were held in Nuremberg, Germany, these trials meant that International Law recognized as inalienable, certain individual human rights.[5]

3. Issued, in 1948, a Universal Declaration of Human Rights.[6]

The Second World War had another lasting impact most relevant to Jamaica. That war, and its aftermath, advanced the decolonization process. The right of people to self-determination was recognized internationally. The weakened state of the old colonial powers also meant they were unable to resist movements towards independence.[7] States in the Pacific, in Africa, the Caribbean, and the Indian subcontinent therefore gained their political independence. The number of states and hence membership of the United Nations increased significantly.

The Sources of International Law

International law is to be found in:[8]

- Treaties

- International custom

- Judicial decisions and teachings of the most highly qualified publicists

- General principles of law

International tribunals, when considering disputes between nations, will have regard to these sources in order to decide what the law is on a particular issue.

A treaty is an agreement between states. Another word for treaty is convention. To be binding, a treaty must be in writing, made between states, intended to be binding, and governed by international law. Such an agreement may involve only two states or it may involve more than two states. If most states of the world are party to a treaty, that treaty can be regarded as establishing an international law binding on all countries, for example, the 1982 Convention on the Law of the Sea,[9] some parts of which bind non-parties. Where several states sign a treaty it is called a multinational treaty. Where only two or a few countries are party to a treaty, that treaty binds only those countries. It is called a bi-lateral or regional treaty.

A publicly issued statement is called a declaration. Sometimes a state or states will issue declarations. These are regarded as non-binding statements of intent or aspiration. The UN General Assembly often issues resolutions, some of which are denoted as declarations. Resolutions by the UN may in some circumstances denote rules of customary international law.

International Law and Human Rights

In order to protect individual human rights many countries sign treaties and issue declarations denoting best practices for law enforcement and other officials.

Jamaica has signed some of these treaties such as:

- The International Covenant on Civil and Political Rights (signed December 19, 1966 ratified October 3, 1975);

- The Convention on The Rights of the Child (signed January 26, 1990 ratified May 14, 1991);

- The Convention on the Elimination of all Forms of Discrimination Against Women (signed July 17, 1980 ratified October 19, 1984), and

- The 1951 Convention Relating to the Status of Refugees (succession July 30, 1964 and acceded to the Protocol on October 30, 1980).

Jamaica is also a party to the Inter American Convention on Human Rights by which Jamaica has agreed to certain standards for its citizens and to their having access to the Inter American Commission on Human Rights.

There are some treaties we have signed but not yet ratified (that is, given effect to in domestic law) such as The Rome Statute of the International Criminal Court. There are others, which Jamaica has neither signed nor ratified, such as The Convention against Torture or other Cruel, Inhumane or Degrading Treatment or Punishment.

Relevant Declarations passed or adopted by the United Nations include:

- The United Nations General Assembly Code of Conduct for Law Enforcement Officials adopted by UN Resolution 34/169 on December 17, 1979;

- United Nations Basic Principles on the Use of Force and Firearms adopted by the 8th United Nations Congress in Havana Cuba, August 27 to September 7, 1990, and

- The United Nations Declaration of Basic Principles of Justice for Victims of Crime and Abuse of Power adopted by General Assembly Resolution 40/34 on November 29, 1985.

The Caribbean Court of Justice (CCJ)

Jamaica is signatory to another important regional treaty. This is the Agreement Establishing the Caribbean Court of Justice. The agreement was signed on February 14, 2001, by twelve Caribbean states. The court created by this agreement has two jurisdictions.

Original Jurisdiction

In the first place it is a court of original jurisdiction designed to resolve all disputes under the Revised Treaty of Chaguaramas, which established the CARICOM Single Market and Economy (a Caribbean free trade area).[10] This involves not only the free movement of goods and services, but the movement of the people of the Caribbean. Jamaica has implemented the original jurisdiction of the Caribbean Court of Justice.[11]

Appellate Jurisdiction

The Caribbean Court of Justice also has an appellate jurisdiction. In this role it functions as the court of final appeal from the national courts of Caribbean states. It is intended that the CCJ will replace the Judicial Committee of the Privy Council in each country's system of courts. Barbados, Guyana, Belize, and Dominica are so far the only

Caribbean nations to have adopted the appellate jurisdiction of the Caribbean Court of Justice.

In order to introduce a new court at the highest level of Jamaica's system of justice a Constitutional amendment process is required.[12] The story of the creation of the Caribbean Court of Justice and the litigation that resulted, has been told elsewhere.[13] The protection given by the Constitution to the courts it creates would be rendered nugatory, not valid, if Parliament could by ordinary legislation, that is with a simple majority vote, create a higher court. Furthermore, unless the new court is entrenched in the Constitution, its continued existence and the right of Jamaicans to appeal to that court could not be guaranteed. This is because a future Parliament could also remove the court by simple legislation. This is contrary to the intention of the framers of Jamaica's Constitution who created for Jamaicans a higher judiciary with constitutionally protected security of tenure.

It may be asked why then was the Judicial Committee of the Privy Council (the Privy Council) not entrenched in our Constitution? There are many reasons. Firstly, the Privy Council was not created by Jamaica. That court existed in England for over two hundred years prior to Jamaica's independence. The Jamaican Constitution merely allowed the right of appeal to continue after independence. Secondly, it would have been unwise (and perhaps impossible) to entrench a court, or the right of appeal to a court, over whose continued existence Jamaica had no control. Thirdly, it was unnecessary to be concerned with protecting the independence from political influence of a court over which, by virtue of its distance, structure and location, no one in Jamaica could have had any influence. The final reason for not entrenching the Privy Council is the fact, as the judges themselves acknowledged, that it is an anachronism.[14]

The CCJ v the UK Privy Council

There is no doubt that the time has come for Jamaica to depart from the Privy Council and to make the CCJ its final court in all civil and criminal cases.[15] Detractors point to the little or no cost to Jamaica of maintaining the Privy Council as compared to the high cost of the CCJ. They say the Privy Council costs the government of Jamaica nothing and is a court of high international reputation, which is attractive to foreign investors. On the other hand appeals to the Privy Council are extremely costly. That court is only available to very wealthy persons and those under sentence of death.[16] The latter receive pro bono legal assistance from English counsel. The CCJ, by virtue of its proximity, is less costly to access. That court is also able to sit in the territory from which an appeal arises. It is also technologically advanced and hence will hear appeals remotely. Another reason for change is that a nation can never be truly independent so long as its former colonial masters, or their agents, have the final say on the law of that nation. Abolition of appeals to the Judicial Committee of the Privy Council is long overdue. That court's continued participation in Jamaica's system of justice is inconsistent with our status as an independent nation.

The Caribbean Court of Justice is a court Jamaica has helped to pay for. It is a court whose judges Jamaica helps to appoint, and it is a court on which Jamaican judges can sit. It is also a court which has performed most creditably.[17]

Conclusion

As an independent state, responsible for its international relations, Jamaica is a proud member of the United Nations and has signed many multinational treaties. Jamaica is committed to the human rights reflected in its Constitution and recognized by international law. Jamaica is also a member of the regional Caribbean Court of Justice but has not yet implemented its appellate jurisdiction.

11.
The Law in Action
– Questions Jamaicans Ask

In previous chapters we described the source of our law, its role and function, as well as how the courts administer that law. In this chapter we answer questions people often ask about the practical application of law in Jamaica today.

What should be the response of a citizen when confronted by a police officer?

It is generally good advice to cooperate with police officers who are carrying out their lawful duty. That lawful duty includes investigating suspicious activity.

Therefore when an officer has reasonable cause to suspect that a crime has been or, is being, or is about to be committed, and has in fact, such an honestly held suspicion, he is entitled to act.

Therefore when an officer has reasonable cause to suspect that a crime has been or, is being, or is about to be committed, and has in fact, such an honestly held suspicion, he is entitled to act.

In an appeal case from the Petty Sessions in the Supreme Court[1] the appellant assaulted a police officer who was arresting him for breaching the Noise Abatement Act.

The facts of that case are interesting. The accused, Mr Gayle, an attorney-at-law was at a location where loud music was being played. A Superintendent of Police having received a credible report that the attorney-at-law was the organizer of the event, asked him his name, and advised him about the report received. The attorney refused to answer any questions and attempted to walk away.

The police officer was therefore lawfully able to arrest the attorney-at-law because the offence (noise-making) was still in progress and the policeman, based upon the information he had received, had an honestly held opinion on reasonable grounds that the person attempting to escape was in fact the perpetrator of an offence under the Noise Abatement Act.

> *Therefore, whereas one has no duty to answer every question posed by a police officer, failure to answer questions in the context of other information the police officer may have can give rise to reasonable suspicion. This can justify an arrest.*

Therefore, whereas one has no duty to answer every question posed by a police officer, failure to answer questions in the context of other information the police officer may have can give rise to reasonable suspicion. This can justify an arrest.

The arrest may be lawful, even if it later turns out the information given to the police officer was inaccurate, so long as it was not unreasonable for the police officer to have an honest belief in its truth.

When a police officer acts without reasonable or probable cause, and without an honestly held belief based on reasonable grounds, the citizen may seek redress or compensation in the civil court. It is usually advisable to obey the instructions of the police officer even as you politely enquire as to the reasonable cause for his instructions and if necessary state your objection.

What is a search warrant?

A warrant is a document issued by the court. It may authorize the search of a person or of property (search warrant), or the arrest of a person (arrest warrant).

A police officer may produce to you a search warrant issued by the courts. If he does so it is your duty to abide by its terms. You should request a copy of the warrant and should read it to satisfy yourself that it is sufficiently specific about the place or person to be searched.

The importance of a warrant and that it should be specific has been endorsed by the Jamaican Court of Appeal in a case[2] where lawyers' offices were searched in circumstances where the warrants were bad for being too general and the legal professional privilege of the lawyer's clients was breached. The court awarded compensation in the form of damages.

> *In another case the police did not rely on a search warrant as the basis to search the claimant's premises and so the court ruled that the legal authority for the search had to be elsewhere.*

In another case,[3] the police did not rely on a search warrant as the basis to search the claimant's premises and so the court ruled that the legal authority for the search had to be elsewhere.

Examples like these show that if, in spite of your objection, the police wrongfully search or stop or otherwise interfere with your liberty (either because they had no valid warrant or because there is no reasonable or probable cause to suspect that an offence has occurred or is about to occur), you can obtain compensation. The citizen should not physically challenge the police officer as it can be dangerous to do so. The thing to do is state your objection and have it recorded. Indicate that your compliance is not voluntary. In that way you will have recourse in the civil courts for breach of your rights under the Constitution. You can also report the incident to INDECOM (see chapter 8).

What are my rights if arrested?

If a police officer arrests you, you have a right to know the reason for the arrest. You also have a right not to incriminate yourself and therefore you are not obliged to answer any questions asked of you. You also have the right to speak with an attorney. In the event you do not have an attorney you should opt to retain 'duty counsel.' These are attorneys, provided by the state at no cost, who will attend and give you advice and representation after your arrest.

What is the difference between an arrest and detention?

At common law an arrest is any deprivation of your liberty. The arrest comes the moment your freedom of movement is restrained. You may therefore be arrested and charged and thereafter brought before the court or you may be arrested and released without charge.

Any unlawful arrest (whether with or without charge) can give rise to a lawsuit against the state for damages. An arrest is unlawful where there was no reasonable cause and / or the officer had no honest belief that there was reasonable cause. In modern times some statutes use the words detain or detention usually with reference to a power to arrest without charge during a state of public emergency or curfew or other extraordinary power. Reasonable cause is always required before effecting an arrest or detention.[4]

What is a Felony?

A felony is a serious crime. Less serious crimes are called misdemeanours. It is often said that there is no power to arrest for a misdemeanor unless it is in progress. A felony can give rise to an arrest on reasonable suspicion even before it has been committed. In the case of misdemeanors which are not in progress, the police should obtain a warrant if they intend to arrest or issue a summons to court if they do not intend to arrest. Typically, misdemeanors are charged on Information and a felony is usually tried on an Indictment.

Does every person arrested have a right to bail?

The correct answer is that everyone has a right to have bail considered. The Constitution of Jamaica[5] provides that any person who is awaiting trial and detained in custody has a right to bail on reasonable conditions *'unless sufficient cause is shown for keeping [that person] in custody.'*

The Bail Act reinforces the principle that a person accused of a crime[6] is presumed innocent until proven guilty. Therefore, punishment should only commence after, not before, conviction for a crime.

However, the law allows for bail to be refused in many circumstances. These include:
  i. *risk of the accused not turning up for his trial;*
  ii. *risk of the accused interfering with the course of justice such as by interfering with witnesses;*
  iii. *prevention of crime, and*
  iv. *the protection of the accused.*

Factors such as the nature and seriousness of the offence may be taken into account when deciding whether bail may be granted.

However, the law[7] allows for bail to be refused in many circumstances. These include:

    i.   risk of the accused not turning up for his trial;

    ii.   risk of the accused interfering with the course of justice such as by interfering with witnesses;

   iii. prevention of crime, and

   iv. the protection of the accused.

Factors such as the nature and seriousness of the offence may be taken into account when deciding whether bail may be granted.[8]

Bail is the facility whereby a person arrested or charged with a crime is allowed to regain his freedom on condition that security (called a recognisance) is provided to ensure he will turn up to court to face his trial. This security may be the payment of cash or a guarantee of payment, or pledging of title to land or property. In the event he does not turn up for court the bond is forfeited and the money or property seized. Sometimes the accused is allowed to provide his own bond but at other times he is required by law to have a person or persons (called a surety or sureties) provide the bond. Bail may be offered by a Justice of the Peace, the police at the police station, or by the judge when the accused is brought before the court.

What is Habeas Corpus?

Habeas Corpus was the process used in the landmark case of Summerset v Stewart (1772). In that case one Granville Sharpe heard that James Somerset, a slave who had escaped from his master in London, was now recaptured and about to be shipped to Jamaica aboard the **Ann and Mary**. *The slave was owned by a customs official, Charles Steuart, who had served in Boston, USA. He had returned to live in London with his trusted, and by all accounts well treated, slave.*

> *James Somerset nevertheless wanted his freedom. Mr Sharpe of the Anti-Slavery Society in England, immediately applied for a Writ of Habeas Corpus to have the ship's Captain John Knowles show cause why (Mr James Somerset) was detained.*

This latin phrase refers to a process whereby anyone detained may be ordered to be brought before the court and an enquiry held into the lawfulness of his or her detention. If there is no reasonable or justifiable cause to detain the person, the judge will order that the person be released.[9]

Habeas Corpus was the process used in the landmark case of *Summerset v Stewart* (1772).[10] In that case one Granville Sharpe heard that James Somerset,[11] a slave who had escaped from his master in London, was now recaptured and about to be shipped to Jamaica aboard the *Ann and Mary*. The slave was owned by a customs official, Charles Steuart,[12] who had served in Boston, USA. He had returned to live in London with his trusted, and by all accounts well treated, slave. James Somerset nevertheless wanted his freedom. Mr Sharpe of the Anti-Slavery Society in England, immediately applied for a Writ of Habeas Corpus to have the ship's Captain John Knowles show cause why (Mr James Somerset) was detained.

In a landmark decision the Lord Chief Justice of England declared that slavery was unknown to the common law. Therefore as there was no legislation creating slavery in England the owner had no right to and could not sell, the slave. He ordered that James Somerset be set free.

In the course of argument, in which the Attorney General of England, insurance companies, and slave owners were involved, it was contended that to declare slavery illegal would severely hurt the British economy. In that context, the Lord Chief Justice reportedly declared, '*Fiat justitia, ruat coelum*' meaning let justice prevail though the heavens may fall.[13]

Does It Make Sense to Sue the Police?

Whenever a person's rights are infringed the appropriate thing to do is seek redress in a court of law. So if your contractual rights are breached you commence a claim for breach of contract or if someone negligently injures you and refuses to compensate you, you should commence a lawsuit. The position is no different when it comes to the state.

The police are agents of the Jamaican state. It is possible to sue the individual police officer (if his identity is known) as well as the government of Jamaica which is often vicariously responsible for his acts or omissions. The Queen personifies the Jamaican state (and its government). The Crown Proceedings Act provides that the Attorney-General should be the named defendant instead of the Queen. Therefore, by law whenever the government of Jamaica is to be sued it is the Attorney-General of Jamaica who is named as the Defendant.

In the 2004 case of *Clinton Bernard v Attorney General*,[14] an off-duty police officer, who refused to wait in line for a

---

In the 2004 case of Clinton Bernard v Attorney General an off-duty police officer, who refused to wait in line for a telephone call at a telephone booth, shot the complainant who objected when the officer attempted to break the queue. The policeman had pretended to be acting in the course of his duty and used his service pistol. The policeman thereafter absconded. Mr Bernard sued the Attorney-General as representing the Crown. The court decided that the Jamaican state was liable to compensate Mr Bernard as, although the policeman was off duty, the state had a duty to ensure its employees did not misuse the awesome power they were given.

---

telephone call at a telephone booth, shot the complainant who objected when the officer attempted to break the queue. The policeman had pretended to be acting in the course of his duty and used his service pistol. The policeman thereafter absconded. Mr Bernard sued the Attorney-General as representing the Crown. The court decided that the Jamaican state was liable to compensate Mr Bernard as, although the policeman was off duty, the state had a duty to ensure its employees did not misuse the awesome power they were given.

Persons should consult an attorney, with a view to obtaining compensation, if the security forces or any other agency of the state wrongfully injures them.

Why do Lawyers represent guilty persons?

This is a commonly asked question. The first point to note is that every person accused of crime is presumed innocent until proved guilty. Proof of guilt occurs in the context of the fair trial guaranteed by the Constitution. This includes a right of access to legal representation.[15] In this regard the attorney-at-law acts on the information (usually called instructions) given to him by his client. It is his duty to put forward his client's case.

Where the client denies the alleged conduct it is for the court, not his own lawyer, to decide if he is speaking the truth or not. The trial is the process by which guilt or innocence is determined.[16]

This lawyer has a duty to advise his client of any legal avenue available for his defence. Some criminal offences, for example, may have statutory time periods or formalities which must be satisfied before a conviction. The lawyer is duty bound to advise his client of them.

The lawyer is also duty bound, without putting forward a positive case, to test the case of the Crown if his client wants him to do that. So, for example, the adequacy of identification evidence may be explored. In the event the Crown cannot prove its case beyond a reasonable doubt the accused is entitled to go free.

Where the client admits his guilt to his attorney, and there is no defence, the attorney has a duty to advise his client that he should either, plead guilty and throw himself on the mercy of the court or, remain silent during his trial where the crown will be 'put to the proof of its case'.

Why should I make a Will?

Whenever persons die property they have left behind can become the subject of bitter dispute.

The Intestate Estates and Property Charges Act was passed to reduce that conflict. It makes detailed provision as to who is to succeed to a person's property where that person dies without making a will. Such a person is said to have died intestate.

A will is a document made by a person to give instructions as to what is to happen to his or her property after death. It is the only way a person can ensure that the property left behind is distributed in the way he or she desires. In the absence of a validly made will, even if you have told others or written a letter, or sent an email, it is the law as set out in the Intestate Estates and Property Charges Act that will apply.

It is therefore advisable always to make a will. You can bequeath specific articles to specific people and even make financial provision for them. It is advisable to have a lawyer advise and prepare a will for you.

A will must have two witnesses to your signature and both witnesses must have been present at the same time to see you sign the will or to see you acknowledge your signature on the will. Witnesses to the will (and their husband or wife) cannot be beneficiaries under the will. It is advisable to appoint executors who will be capable of seeing that your wishes as expressed in the will are carried out. It is always advisable to let the persons know you are selecting them to be executors. You should keep the original of the will in a secure place and leave a copy with the attorney who made the will or with a trusted person such as the executor.

What to do if someone dies at home

If someone dies elsewhere than in a hospital the police should be called before the body is removed. If possible, it is adviseable to call the deceased's medical doctor to attend and pronounce the cause of death. If the person was at the time not under medical care it may be difficult to have a doctor attend. Therefore, the coroner for the parish or the chief medical officer may be required to conduct an enquiry. A post mortem examination, popularly called an autopsy, will be done as part of the investigation if the death is sudden and the cause unknown, or there is reasonable cause to suspect death was violent or unnatural or that a medical certificate as to cause of death will not be obtained. Upon receiving the report from the medical examiner the coroner, or the relevant police officer, may authorize the burial of the body. After receiving the police report and the medical report on the post mortem, the coroner will summon a jury and commence an inquest which is a hearing to consider evidence. The coroner and a jury will then hear evidence and say whether or not anyone may be criminally responsible for the death. The Coroner's inquest is not a trial so no one will then be convicted.[17]

What do I do if involved in a motor vehicle accident?

Any driver of a motor vehicle who is involved in a collision has a duty to report it to the police. When you do so you should record the name and number of the police officer taking the report even if it is an officer who attends the scene of the accident. This will assist in proving you made a report and it is information your insurer will find useful. You should always exchange particulars of name, address, insurance company, and policy numbers with the other driver involved. You should also report the accident to your own insurance company as soon as possible. If you do not do so you may be in breach of your policy of insurance.

If you are a passenger in a vehicle involved in an accident, you should also obtain the details of the drivers, vehicle owners, and insurance company insuring each motor vehicle. This will be necessary if you are to pursue a claim for any injury or loss you incurred as a result of the accident.

Sometimes, if the damage is minor, the other driver may offer to have it fixed. Even if you are minded to allow this you should still report the accident to the police and to your insurers and explain that the other person has offered to pay to have your vehicle fixed. You should also have the intended repairer acknowledge in writing that he is looking to the other person for payment and not to you. Therefore, in the event the repairer is not paid, he will not exercise his repairers' lien[18] on your vehicle.

What is Insurance?

The law related to insurance is detailed and complicated. Insurance refers to the coverage of risk. Typically, it is a person (the insurer) who agrees, in exchange for a relatively small payment, to compensate another (the insured) in the event of a particular loss. It is a way of socially sharing the burden of loss.

Insurance law is concerned primarily with the interpretation of the insurance contract. There are some basic principles, for example, the insured person has a duty of honest disclosure to the insurance company. A failure to be honest when completing the proposal for insurance can therefore result in loss of coverage.[19]

There are some types of insurance that the law requires persons to have. The Motor Vehicle Insurance (Third Party Risks) Act says every motor vehicle owner must have it insured for damage to third parties.

Why do we need a jury?

Trial by jury is a feature of the common law system.[20] The jury is comprised of ordinary men and women whose duty it is to consider the evidence and decide the facts of the case. The jury is an institutional bar to tyranny as justice is not administered entirely by agents of the state.

There are some who regard the jury system as unnecessary because it is susceptible to bribery, corruption, intimidation, and in small societies like ours bias. Such persons sometimes point to Civil Law countries which operate justice systems without jurors.

The better view is that this participation by ordinary citizens enures to greater public confidence in the results of a trial. Many Civil Law countries have built in safeguards such as having 'assessors' sit to assist their trial judges. Others have more than one judge sit to try criminal cases and on appeal allow the appellate court to rehear the evidence.

Trial by jury, and the precautions in the Civil Law jurisdiction, ensure that guilt or innocence is not determined by a single judge who, after all, is only human.

12.
Crime, Democracy, and the Way Forward[1]

Jamaica boasts beautiful beaches, abundant rivers, verdant mountains, and unique flora and fauna, all of which attract millions of tourists each year. The country has changed governments democratically at regular intervals since 1944. Its written Constitution guarantees basic human rights to all persons. This island of 2.8 million people can boast of a free press, multiple media houses, and an independent judiciary.

Jamaica: Crime Capital?

All this notwithstanding, rather than peace and serenity, it is crime and violence which bedevil the society. Jamaica's murder rate outstrips that of most countries in the world. In 2016 one pundit[2] asserted that Jamaica was the fourth most violent country on earth. Private security firms are retained by those who can afford it as confidence in the state's ability to protect wanes. Those who can't afford it seek to protect themselves by other means. The formal structures to provide justice don't seem to be coping. External pressure on the island's institutions come in part from the hundreds of criminal deportees sent to Jamaica each year primarily by the United States and England. The narcotics trade, ready availability of illegal firearms and fallout from scamming and other organized crime, also threaten to overwhelm Jamaica's justice and national security apparatus. Crime now impacts Jamaica's ability to grow the economy.[3]

Human rights organizations and activists are sometimes scapegoated for the crime, violence, and murder in Jamaica. A reverend gentleman was reported as describing them as 'human wrong activists' and a noted police officer, now retired, repeatedly referred to human rights activists as criminal rights advocates. This blame game is understandable and is not unique to Jamaica. Countries in crisis often witness the silencing of those who stand for truth, justice, and democracy. It is often a prelude to the harsh measures and deprivation of rights that totalitarians apply in order to secure peace and stability.

Successive governments have, since independence, endeavoured to fight a war on crime using the tried and failed methods of the past. These consist of arbitrary, and therefore illegal, stopping and searching of pedestrians and motorists;[4] raids, cordons, and searches in which hundreds of young men are herded into corrals for processing, and periodic invasion of certain communities by way of major operations. States of public emergency (SOEs) have been declared and draconian anti-crime legislation enacted from time to time.[5] Such measures may briefly stabilize or slow the crime wave, but the rate of violent crime usually rebounds once the shock and awe of the measures subside. There have been some useful initiatives such as the creation of an independent commission (INDECOM)[6] to investigate allegations against the security forces. This has helped to restore public trust and confidence in the police force and has resulted in a marked reduction in extra judicial killings. The effort to combine social improvement in communities with aggressive policing (the ZOSO initiative) is also a step in the right direction.[7]

Reasons for the Culture of Violence

In the search for solutions it is appropriate to consider how and why Jamaica arrived at this point. Poverty alone cannot explain it as there are poorer nations in the world, many with larger populations, but with less violent crime. Neither are slavery and colonialism sufficient explanations because many post-colonial slave societies do not have the *endemic* violence seen in Jamaica.[8]

Jamaica has been plagued by violence and crime since the days of colonialism. Statistics from Jonathan Dolby's *Crime and Punishment in Jamaica*,[9] show that in the years 1756–1856 homicides averaged 5 per year. In the period 1880–1915 the average was 20 per year. In 1915–1958 it was 25 to 30 per year. There was a steady increase. The rate of murder per one hundred thousand of the population does not present a pretty picture. In 1773 the island's total population was estimated at 216,000, at an average 5 per year, the rate would be 2.3 homicides per 100,000. In 1901 with a population of 756,000 adopting the average of 20 per year the rate killed per hundred thousand would be 2.6. In 2020 with a population of 2.8 million people the rate per one hundred thousand was 46.5, the region's highest.[10] Efforts to blame today's high rate of violent crime on conditions in the post-independence era also ignore the many violent upheavals of the past and the even more violent and repressive measures adopted to suppress them. The historical accounts of the noted highwaymen, *Three Finger Jack* of St Thomas and *Plato* of Westmoreland, remind us that robbery and murder were features of life in eighteenth century Jamaica.[11] It is also a fact that *political* violence predated the twentieth century so, for example, in the election of 1851 in the parish of St David (now part of St Thomas) it was reported:

One candidate arrived with some thirty supporters...His rival was supported by a crowd of 300 men, most of whom were armed with a bludgeon...a riot developed...and in the ensuing tumult the clerk of the vestry was killed.[12]

Jamaica's *culture* of violence is no surprise given the brutal way in which the island nation developed and the progressive and continuing separation in almost all spheres of activity of those who have from those who have not. When Christopher Columbus arrived he is reported to have declared that the native inhabitants 'would make good servants'. This is what the Spanish set out to make of them. Upon the Taínos being decimated by war and disease, the Spanish enslaved and imported Africans. The brutality of slave society and its institutions increased exponentially after the English captured Jamaica from the Spanish. Firstly, because Jamaica had a larger proportion of absentee owners whose estates were run by agents/overseers, there was no incentive to educate, or otherwise preserve the well-being of their masters' property, replacements for which were readily available.[13] Secondly, the freed Africans (Maroons), left behind by the Spanish, waged war against the English for approximately one hundred years in order to preserve their freedom,[14] and thirdly, because treaties of peace with the Maroons did not bring an end to violent slave insurrection and revolt as the English had hoped. Jamaica's mountainous terrain and verdant forests offered a relatively safe and viable alternative to life on the hated plantation. The end of slavery, by way of the Emancipation Act of 1833, was propelled as much by the advocacy of antislavery societies as by the many slave revolts culminating in the monumental Christmas Rebellion of 1831/32 led by Samuel Sharpe.[15]

Post slavery Jamaica did not offer much improvement by way of economic or political advancement, for the emancipated. The planters were compensated to the tune of millions of pounds by the British government but most of that money remained right there in the mother country where many absentee owners lived.[16] But for a rather inadequate *Education Grant* made to the colony, there was no provision for the economic or social well-being of the newly freed men, women and children who formed the overwhelming majority of the population. The institution of slavery, it must be remembered, had systematically attempted to dehumanize and keep dependent these individuals. It had discouraged stable family life, religious instruction and the education of these persons. Males were studs and nothing more. The resultant poverty, unhealthy attitudes to family life, parental irresponsibility, and anti-social attitudes have been passed down from generation to generation.[17]

The planter class, after emancipation, used tax and other laws in an oppressive manner in an attempt to keep the now free persons tied to the plantation. Jamaica had much arable and available Crown lands and many of the emancipated fled the estate to establish villages and smallholdings and to live in and around town centres.[18] The rebellion of 1865 in St Thomas was as much a result of the economic and social conditions, as it was of the injustices in a society favouring the minority ruling planter class.

Crown Colony government, which succeeded the voluntary dissolution of the elected assembly in 1866 (because the ruling class resisted socio-economic and political reform), did not do nearly enough for the education and economic welfare of the vast majority of Jamaicans. Trade union activity and the political turmoil of the 1930s and '40s, resulted in a gradual increase in civic participation by the Black majority. However, this did not create a more equitable distribution of the island's wealth.

Independence came in 1962, but the hoped for economic empowerment has not materialized. In the six decades since then, inadequate resources have been allocated to properly educate and train all our people. Access to the best schools, at the basic and primary level, is restricted to the relative few who can afford to pay for it. The implementation of free education at the primary and secondary levels has done much to ameliorate the situation. However, access to the best quality education continues to mirror, and therefore perpetuate the haves and have-not divide. Similarly, inadequate efforts have been made to facilitate the people's social and economic advancement through access to capital. Profligate borrowing, irresponsible spending, and economic downturn have no doubt rendered these tasks harder for successive governments in independent Jamaica.

Political changes have occurred but the promise, which is epitomized in our national anthem's refrain *Justice, truth be ours forever*, was not kept. It seems that for the better part of the last sixty years principle has been sacrificed on the altar of popularity.[19] Truth was the first casualty, and with truth went any hope of justice. Indeed, the general failure of our system of justice has been a catalyst for Jamaica's spiralling rate of murder. The calculated rate of return for crime compares favourably, in the criminal mind, to the relatively low chance of being punished. Unlawful detentions by police officers, the net-fishing approach to crime solving, the beatings in the lock-up, extrajudicial killings, as well as the profitable but illegal drug trade, have all helped to alienate people and foster a significant underworld, which has little regard for established institutions. Until all of this is understood, prescriptions for a solution to crime and violence will miss the mark.

Prescription for Change

Any approach to the problem has therefore to be both pragmatic and holistic. It must be such as to affect attitudes and behavioural norms. If it does not, Jamaica will slide into anarchy or end up with a revolutionary dictatorship ruled by a strong man who provides peace and security. This scenario has occurred in other post-colonial societies and unless the appropriate correctives are taken, Jamaica will be no exception.

Jamaica's crime problem is not only a law enforcement issue although, obviously, policing has its place. In order to become a society of peace, with moderate to low crime, we must first create an environment of economic, social, and political justice for all. This, after all, is what the rule of law in its widest sense entails. The data, and scientific study, suggest that crime suppression measures will not by themselves solve Jamaica's problem of crime and violence.[20] To be successful, any plan of action should be consistent with the human rights guaranteed by our Constitution and as a pragmatic, holistic solution, involve the following:

- *Reintegration of the alienated and in particular the urban ghetto youth.* This requires a concerted effort among state funded agencies, the private sector, the church, and other community based organizations, as well as the police. Trade training opportunities and capital for small projects should be provided. Persons with good ideas should not have access to venture capital or other resources denied merely because of where they live.

- *Restructuring the role, function, and organization of the Police force.* Professor Anthony Harriott has written extensively on the subject.[21] Policing should be firm but fair. The several special squads should be disbanded and placed on regular police duties and a rapid response unit created in their place. This very mobile force must comprise members of the military who have the discipline, training and mobility to respond by land, sea or air whenever the officer on the beat requires assistance. Any violent confrontation in the island will thereby be met with a swift, immediate, and professional response. This is not a proposal to merge the police and the army, as this will merely compromise the efficiency, discipline, and esprit de corps of our military. The Second Battalion Jamaica Regiment has approximately 1,000 men. This suffices to ensure three operational bases located throughout the island with three eight hour shifts of 100 men per shift, thus ensuring a 24-hour state of readiness of the rapid response unit.

Alongside this initiative must be a boosting of policing methods, using undercover operatives and improved technology. There needs to be expansion of community policing, that is, the beat and foot patrol. The police presence must be seen regularly and not in the form of periodic invading armies. Police officers on the beat must have zones of responsibility in preference to the static duty often employed. The beat officers should be regularly briefed and debriefed by the Criminal Investigation Branch. The police must operate independently of the political arm. The time has come to give the Commissioner of Police constitutional security of tenure, after putting in place an independent and transparent appointment process. A meaningful effort to bring delinquent police officers to justice is required. This will restore public confidence. The police must be held to professional standards

127

whether or not the DPP has opted to prosecute and whether or not there is a conviction.

- *Offender rehabilitation and reintegration.* The rate at which prisoners return to prison (called recidivism) in Jamaica's prison system is approximately 30 per cent.[22] Only a small percentage of inmates in our penal institutions access rehabilitation programmes. Additional resources should be used to develop noncustodial methods of punishment, expand rehabilitation measures, and ameliorate the existing facilities. An ex-convict should have a trade and a hope that better can be achieved. Repeat offenders should be given longer sentences. The parole system should be overhauled.

- *Enhanced efficiency in the system of Justice.* There is no magic wand. Until adequate resources are dedicated to improve the justice system, for example, in the construction of new courthouses, a hard look at centuries old systems and approaches should be taken. The system of justice needs to be overhauled. If justice delayed is justice denied, then justice has been denied to Jamaicans for a long time. There have been many studies and recommendations and over the years there have been changes to some procedures such as the introduction of case management and other initiatives. However, what is needed is a comprehensive implementation of the many recommendations. Our courts need to become efficient and the use of technology more effective. The time has come for the police to be relieved of court duties. Court security services, including the service and execution of its processes, should be provided by a separate body specially trained and under the command of the Chief Justice. This will enhance the independence of the judiciary and free up more officers for policing duties.

- *Values and Attitudes.* A sustained campaign to reverse habits instilled and passed from generation to generation is perhaps the least costly but most difficult to institute. Responsible parenting, rights and duties of the citizen, dispute resolution through dialogue, and the relevance of the Rule of Law, should be the areas of focus. The schools, churches, places of employment, prisons, and our political representatives should all be involved. Increased investment in early childhood education will improve the prospect of positive socialization and upward mobility for our people.

Constitutional Change?

After sixty years it is perhaps time to reflect on the need for change to Jamaica's Constitution.[23] Although the present structure has functioned without any of the explosive changes that occurred in many other post colonial societies, amendments may enhance public confidence.

The time may have come to give certain institutions and persons appointed to them, constitutionally guaranteed security of tenure. At the same time, the method of appointment of persons to these institutions should be improved upon to allow for fairness and transparency. These institutions include the Electoral Commission, the Integrity Commission, and the Office of the Public Defender. The time may also have come to give constituents the power to recall members of parliament with whom they are out of favour. It may be time to broaden the skillsets available to the Prime Minister when appointing the Cabinet by enabling appointments from among persons other than members of the parliament.

These changes and others may be necessary to re-engage the public interest and retain public confidence in our system of governance.

Conclusion

In summary, Jamaica's spiralling rate of violent crime can, if not reversed, undermine its law and legal system. This will in turn destabilize the Jamaican economy. A failing economy will further increase the propensity to crime and lead to an ever spiralling cycle. It is testimony to the durability of the Jamaican Constitution, its institutions, and the resilience of Jamaicans, that notwithstanding the steady increase in criminal activity, the Jamaican state has not yet failed.

A culture of violence, which took 400 years to create, will not be undone overnight. In order to secure a free, productive, democratic, and peaceful future, human rights must be respected as Jamaicans tackle crime, corruption, and violence. The objective must be to create a society which is peaceful, fair, just, and equitable for all.

Our country, notwithstanding its challenges will continue to be enriched so long as we maintain the rule of law, respect for our Constitution and, national pride in our institutions.[24]

Notes

Chapter 1 – Introduction

1.   See *Hemans v A-G* [2013] JMSC Civil 75; (award of damages varied on appeal in *A-G v Hemans* [2015] JMCA Civ 63).

Chapter 2 – The Law and Legal Systems of the World

1.   H. Patrick Glenn, *Legal Traditions of the World: Sustainable Diversity in Law,* 4th ed. (Oxford: Oxford University Press, 2010).
2.   See chapter 11 for more on the jury system.
3.   K. W. Patchett, 'Reception of Law in the West Indies' *Jamaica Law Journal* (1972): 17.
4.   Karl Marx, 'Critique of the Gotha Programme, 1876', as quoted by John Eaton in *Political Economy: A Marxist Textbook* (International Publishers Co. Inc., 1966), 253.
5.   Rose-Marie Belle Antoine, *Commonwealth Caribbean Law and Legal Systems*, 2nd ed. (Oxfordshire: Routledge-Cavendish, 2006).

Chapter 3 – How Jamaica Received its Legal System

1.   Phillip Sherlock and Hazel Bennett, *The Story of the Jamaican People* (Kingston: Ian Randle Publishers, 1998), 42–50.

2. Karl Watson, 'Amerindian Cave Art in Jamaica' *Jamaica Journal* Vol. 21 No.1 (February to April 1988): 13–17.

3. Genoa, then a city state, now a part of Italy, partnered with Portugal to sponsor trading and to navigate the African coast.

4. Sherlock and Bennett, *The Story of the Jamaican People*, 56.

5. Sherlock and Bennett, *The Story of the Jamaican People*, 55–62.

6. In 1611 there were 523 Spaniards, 558 slaves, 107 free Blacks, 74 Taíno herdsmen and 75 newcomers. See Sherlock and Bennett, *The Story of the Jamaican People*, 74.

7. Sherlock and Bennett, *The Story of the Jamaican People*, 68.

8. For a detailed account of the English conquest of Jamaica, see Carey Robinson, *Fight For Freedom: The Destruction of Slavery in Jamaica* (Kingston: LMH Publishing Company, 2007), 10–27.

9. See chapter 2.

10. *Campbell v Hall* (1558–1774) All ER Rep. 252.

11. For modern applications of the reception rules see, *R v Commissioner of Police and others ex parte Cephas #2* (1976) 15 JLR 3, and *Lance Melbourne v Christina Wan* (1985) 22 JLR 131. See also discussion in *Commonwealth Caribbean Law and Legal Systems* 2nd edition by Professor Rose-Marie Belle Antoine (London: Routledge-Cavendish Publishers Ltd, 2008), 73–92, and in *Historical Foundations of Jamaican Law* by Raphael Codlin (Kingston: Canoe Press, 2003), 1–6. Jamaica's reception date is, by statute, now 1728.

12. Lloyd G. Barnett, *Constitutional Law of Jamaica* (Oxford: Oxford University Press, 1977), 3.

13. Jamaica also benefited from the activities of privateers/
pirates (who became known as the Buccaneers) between
1657 and 1692, when an earthquake sank most of
Port Royal to the bottom of the sea. Detailed accounts
can be found in Anthony Gambrill, *In Search of the
Buccaneers* (London: Macmillan Caribbean, 2007),
chapter 4 and David Howard, *Kingston* (Kingston: Ian
Randle Publishers, 2004), 35–45.

14. A Spaniard, Pedro de Mazuela, is credited, in 1534,
with being one of the first to recognize the profitability
of sugar cane cultivation in Jamaica. Sherlock and
Bennett, *The Story of the Jamaican People*, 69.

15. See *Summerset v Stewart* (1772) 98 ER 499; and
Steven M. Wise, *Though the Heavens May Fall: The
Landmark Trial That Led to the End of Human Slavery*
(Boston, MA: De Capo Press, 2006). Some, like F. O.
Shyllon, *Black Slaves in Britain 1774* (Oxford: Oxford
University Press, 1974), take a less charitable view of
Lord Mansfield's judgment. It is irrefutable, however,
that case or common law is always subject to statute
law. Lord Mansfield was therefore correct in saying
that there was no statute in England giving effect
to enslavement (as distinct from serfdom) and that
common law principles did not do so. The fact that he
later tried to downplay the general applicability of this
decision does not detract from the correctness of the
legal principle stated.

16. The full history of the Maroons is told by Bev Carey,
*The Maroon Story: The Authentic and Original History
of the Maroons in the History of Jamaica 1490–1880*
(Kingston: Agouti Press, 1997). A detailed account of
the Maroon Wars is provided in Carey Robinson, *The
Iron Thorn: The Defeat of the British by the Jamaican
Maroons* (Kingston: LMH Publishing Company, 1993).

17. See *R v Man O Rowe* [1956] 7 JLR 45 and Stephen Vasciannie, 'Law and the Maroon State', *Sunday Observer*, January 9, 2022.
18. See chapter 2.
19. For a comprehensive consideration of the interplay between Executive authority and Parliamentary power see the two 'Brexit' decisions of the UK's highest court in: *R(On Application of Miller & Anor) v Secretary of State for Exiting The European Union* [2017] 1 All ER 593 and, *R (on the application of Miller) (Appellant) v The Prime Minister (Respondent); Cherry and others (Respondents) v Advocate General for Scotland (Appellant) (Scotland)* [2019] UKSC 41 (judgment delivered September 24, 2019).

Chapter 4 – Constitutional Development and the Road to Independence

1. Royal Proclamation, 14 December 1661 C.O. 1/15ff181-184 and C.O. 139/1f8, as quoted in Lloyd G. Barnett, *Constitutional Law of Jamaica* (Oxford: Oxford University Press, 1977).
2. See Barnett, *Constitutional Law of Jamaica,* 2; and Philip Sherlock and Hazel Bennett, *The Story of the Jamaican People* (Kingston: Ian Randle Publishers, 1998), 85–87.
3. For an account see Sherlock and Bennett, *The Story of the Jamaican People*, 86-87.
4. Barnett, *Constitutional Law of Jamaica*, 2–4; and Sherlock and Bennett, *The Story of the Jamaican People*, 87.
5. See *Campbell v Hall* (1558–1774) All ER Rep. 252.
6. 'Journal of the House of Assembly vol 1 app, 22–23' as quoted by Barnett, *Constitutional Law of Jamaica*, 4.
7. See Dennis Morrison, 'The Reception of English Law in Jamaica' *West Indian Law Journal* (October 1979):

43, an article cited by the Jamaican Court of Appeal in *Brown v Jamaica National Building Society* [2010] JMCA Civ.7 (unreported judgment dated March 4, 2010) and K. W. Patchett, 'Reception of Law in the West Indies' (1972) *Jamaica Law Journal* 17.

8. See chapter 3 for a discussion of the reception rules.

9. For a detailed discussion of the system of governance in the period see William A. Green, *British Slave Emancipation: The Sugar Colonies and the Great Experiment, 1830–1865* (Oxford: Oxford University Press, 1976), chapter 3.

10. Eric Williams, *Capitalism and Slavery* (London: Andre Deutsch Limited, 1964), 136.

11. Sherlock and Bennett, *The Story of the Jamaican People*, 92–93; Barnett, *Constitutional Law*, 5.

12. Williams, *Capitalism and Slavery*, chapter 4, gives a graphic account of their wealth and political influence.

13. See Sherlock and Bennett, *The Story of the Jamaican People*, 134–49; Carey Robinson, *Fight For Freedom: The Destruction of Slavery in Jamaica*, 2nd ed. (Kingston: Kingston Publishers Limited, 1993), 55–85; and Carey Robinson, *The Iron Thorn: The Defeat of the British by the Jamaican Maroons* (Kingston: Kingston Publishers, 1993) for detailed expositions of the Maroon Wars and slave revolts.

14. Williams, *Capitalism and Slavery*, 135–53 details this development. See also Sherlock and Bennett, *The Story of the Jamaican People*, 176–211; and Green, *British Slave Emancipation*, 43–58.

15. *Summerset v Stewart* (1772) 98 ER 499.

16. Steven M. Wise, *Though the Heavens May Fall: The Landmark Trial That Led to the End of Human Slavery* (Boston, MA: De Capo Press, 2005), 217–25; chapter 3, note 14; and Robinson, *Fight For Freedom*, 123–24.

17. Sherlock and Bennett, *The Story of the Jamaican People*, 229–30.

18. See Sherlock and Bennett, *The Story of the Jamaican People*, 212–18; Green, *British Slave Emancipation*, 112–27; and Robinson, *Fight for Freedom*, 151–62, for detailed accounts of the Western Liberation Uprising of 1831–32 and its far reaching consequences.

19. Robinson, *Fight for Freedom*, 160.

20. See Green, *British Slave Emancipation*, 118–27 for a discussion of how the system was structured, and 129–61 for how it functioned.

21. Sherlock and Bennett, *The Story of the Jamaican People*, 159 and 230; and Green, *British Slave Emancipation*, 59–64 and 119. At the time of emancipation 80 per cent of plantation owners were absentees. The compensation paid to Jamaican slave owners was £6,616,927, of the £20,000,000 for the empire.

22. Barnett, *Constitutional Law*, 6–7.

23. See Sherlock and Bennett, *The Story of the Jamaican People*, 246–62; Clinton A. Hutton, *Colour for Colour Skin for Skin: Marching with the Ancestral Spirits into War Oh at Morant Bay* (Kingston: Ian Randle Publishers, 2015), 120–42; and, Robinson, *Fight for Freedom*, 131–62 for the account of his political and pastoral work.

24. Barnett, *Constitutional Law*, 7.

25. Gad Heuman, *The Killing Time: The Morant Bay Rebellion Jamaica* (London: Macmillan Education Limited, 1994), 170–77 details the consequences for Governor Eyre. See also Devon Dick, *The Cross and the Machete: Native Baptists of Jamaica – Identity, Ministry and Legacy* (Kingston: Ian Randle Publishers, 2010); Green, *British Slave Emancipation*; Sherlock

and Bennett, *The Story of the Jamaican People,* 257–62; and Hutton, *Colour for Colour,* for useful historical accounts of the rebellion (some historians call it a war).

26. Sherlock and Bennett, *The Story of the Jamaican People,* 264–66; and Tracy Robinson, Arif Bulkan and Adrian Saunders, *Fundamentals of Caribbean Constitutional Law* (London: Sweet and Maxwell, 2021), 24–27.

27. Barnett, *Constitutional Law,* 10.

28. Sherlock and Bennett, *The Story of the Jamaican People,* 372–88 and Barnett, *Constitutional Law,* 15–23 provide detailed expositions of the process of decolonization.

29. See Sherlock and Bennett, *The Story of the Jamaican People,* 283–291 for an outline of the work of Dr Love, and 292–315 for the work of Marcus Garvey.

30. See Patrick E. Bryan and Karl Watson, *Not For Wages Alone: Eyewitness Summaries of the 1938 Labour Rebellion in Jamaica* (Kingston: The Social History Project, Dept of History & Archaeology, UWI, 2003), for eyewitness accounts of these events.

31. Barnett, *Constitutional Law,* 15–16.

32. See chapter 10, note 7.

33. See Barnett, *Constitutional Law,* 24–33; Robinson et al. *Fundamentals of Caribbean Constitutional Law,* 35–39; and Edward Seaga, *My Life and Leadership, Volume 1: Clash of Ideologies* (London: Macmillan, 2010), 45–86 for details.

34. Seaga, *My Life and Leadership,* 98.

35. Michael Manley, *Jamaica: Struggle in the Periphery* (London: Third World Media, 1983), 33–34.

36. M. G. Smith, *Plural Society in the British West Indies* (Kingston: Sangster's Bookstores limited in association with Berkley, CA: University of California Press, 1965), 162–75.

37. Sherlock and Bennett, *The Story of the Jamaican People*, 399.
38. Barnett, *Constitutional Law*, 24.
39. *DPP v Nasralla* (1967) 10 JLR 1, at 5F.
40. See chapter 6.
41. See Robinson et al., *Fundamentals of Caribbean Constitutional Law*, 51–52, and their critique of the constitution-making process at 59–63.
42. Barnett, *Constitutional Law*, 32–33.
43. Arguably, these disappointments fuelled civil disturbance in the 1960s and the populist socialist experiment of the 1970s.

Chapter 5 – *Sources of Jamaican Law*

1. See chapter 4.
2. The Constitution does not define Her Majesty, nor does it have any express provision creating a monarch. The Jamaica (Constitution) Order in Council 1962 was however made at Buckingham Palace and recites that it is made by 'The Queen's Most Excellent Majesty in Council her Majesty'. There is therefore little doubt that the reference is to the reigning monarch of the United Kingdom. See Lloyd G. Barnett, *The Constitutional Law of Jamaica* (Oxford: Oxford University Press, 1977), 162–66.
3. The Constitution, section 68(1) and (2).
4. The Governor-General's Privy Council must not be confused with the Judicial Committee of the Privy Council in England; see page 43 in this chapter.
5. The Constitution of Jamaica, section 90.
6. The Constitution of Jamaica, section 69.
7. The Constitution of Jamaica, sections 94(6) and 125(5).
8. The Constitution of Jamaica, section 34.
9. The Constitution of Jamaica, section 36.

10. The Constitution of Jamaica, section 35.
11. The Constitution of Jamaica, section 80(1) and (2). Being the person who in the Governor-General's judgment, 'is best able to command a majority of those who do not support the Government or, if there is no such person, the member of that House who in his judgment commands the support of the largest single group of such members who are prepared to support one leader'.
12. The Constitution of Jamaica, sections 98 (Chief Justice), 104 (President of Court of Appeal), 111 (Judicial Services Commission), 124 (Public Service Commission), 129 (Police Service Commission).
13. One opposition leader reportedly said he would, 'organize, organize, organize and oppose, oppose, oppose'. See Dorian H. Francis, *Jamaica Observer* Sunday, March 22, 2020.
14. Barnett, *Constitutional Law*, 218–19.
15. As to the meaning of entrenched provision see page 37–38. *(under Separation of Powers)*
16. The Constitution of Jamaica, sections 97–109.
17. The Constitution of Jamaica, sections 98(1) and 104 (1).
18. *Hinds v R* (1976) 24 WIR 326, and Tracy Robinson, Arif Bulkan and Adrian Saunders, *Fundamentals of Caribbean Constitutional Law* (London: Sweet and Maxwell, 2021), 301 and 314.
19. The Constitution of Jamaica, section 49.
20. For discussion on what is a Bill see page 39.
21. The Constitution of Jamaica, section 61(3).
22. The Constitution of Jamaica, section 49(2),(3),(5) and (6); usually a total of 6 months.
23. *Marbury v Madison* (1803) Cranch 137 (decision of the United States Supreme Court); *Hinds v R* (1976) 24

WIR 326, (a decision of the Judicial Committee of the Privy Council); and, *Collymore v AG* (1967) 12 WIR 5 (a decision of the Court of Appeal of Trinidad and Tobago).

24. The Constitution of Jamaica, section 1(9), section 19 (1) and (3) and section 20(5).

25. *Sabaroche v The Speaker of the House of Assembly* (1999) 60 WIR 235.

26. *Bahamas Methodist Church v Symonette* [2000] 5LRC 196 (PC Bah).

27. See, for example, *Hinds v R*; and *Julian J. Robinson v The Attorney General of Jamaica* [2019] JMFC Full 4 (unreported judgment delivered April 12, 2019).

28. See Rose-Marie Belle Antoine, *Commonwealth Caribbean Law and Legal Systems*, 2nd ed. (Oxfordshire: Routledge-Cavendish, 2006), 243–86 for a detailed discussion.

29. See *In re Estate Carlton Roy Campbell, Winsome Bennett v The Ministry of Finance, The Jamaica Constabulary Force and The Attorney General of Jamaica* 2012 HCV 00634 (unreported judgment of Campbell J dated December 11, 2015) in which a purposive approach was used to determine the meaning of the word spouse.

30. See the judgment of Sykes J (as he then was) in *Petal Murray v Kenneth Neita* (2006) HCV 0176 (unreported judgment dated August 18, 2006).

31. See Law Reporting at page 41–42.

32. The Lord Chancellor was head of the Judiciary and roughly equivalent to the Chief Justice in Jamaica today with the important difference that in England the Lord Chancellor also sat as a member of the cabinet and was keeper of the Royal Seal. In 2005 there were substantial reforms in England which transferred the Lord Chancellor's judicial role to separate office holders.

Today the Lord Chancellor roughly approximates to a Minister of Justice in Jamaica.

33. Antoine, *Commonwealth Caribbean Law and Legal Systems*, 166–76 for a discussion of the development of the Law of Equity.

34. Judicature (Supreme Court) Act, sections 4, 27, and 48.

35. www.supremecourt.gov.jm and www.courtofappeal. gov.jm

36. For a discussion of *stare decisis* see, *A1 Limited v Mary Grace Abrahams* [2019] JMSC Civ 3 (unreported judgment of Batts J on January 25, 2019).

37. See, Stephen Vasciannie, 'The Privy Council versus The Caribbean Court of Appeal', Cultural Studies Initiative, Office of the Deputy Vice Chancellor, UWI (1996), 4–5, and The Position Paper of the Jamaican Bar Association on the Proposed Caribbean Court of Appeal (unpublished) cited in David Batts, 'Judicial Independence, the Jamaican Bar Association and IJCHR & others v Attorney General Jamaica' *West Indian Law Journal* Vol. 31 (May & October 2006): 115.

38. See discussion under Separation of Powers at page 37–38.

39. A Revenue Court was created in 1972 to handle revenue appeals. The practice and procedure applicable to the civil division of the Supreme Court applies to the Revenue Court which is therefore regarded as a part of its Civil Division. A Supreme Court Judge is appointed to sit in the Revenue Court, appeals from which go to the Court of Appeal.

40. See chapter 7 for a closer discussion on the civil and criminal divisions of the Supreme Court.

41. The Criminal Justice (Administration) Act, section 11a (as amended by the Jury (Amendment) Act 2015).

42. This was changed by the Judicature (Resident Magistrates) (Amendment and Change of Name) Act, 2016.

43. In some parishes there is a court specially designed to handle matters related to children. This Family Court is a court of record staffed by a parish court judge, see the Judicature (Family Court) Act of 1975.

44. Barnett, *Constitutional Law*, 319.

45. *Donoghue v Stevenson* [1932] AC 562 in which Lord Atkin articulated the 'good neighbour principle'.

46. An order preventing a party from dissipating, or removing assets from the country, in order to evade the court's process. It is also called a freezing order. See *Mareva Compania Naveria S.A.* [1975] 2 Lloyds law Reports 509 and *Nippon Yusen Kaisha v Karageorgis* [1975] 1 WLR 1093. Justice Laing of the Jamaican Supreme Court explains its origin and purpose in the case of *Hasheba Development Company Limited v Petroleum Corporation of Jamaica Limited et al.* [2021] JMCC Comm 10 (unreported judgment dated March 12, 2021.

47. But see Antoine's thought provoking discussion in *Commonwealth Caribbean Law and Legal Systems*, 177–200.

48. 7 WIR 118.

49. At page 129F of the report; and see *O'Brien Loans Ltd v Missick* (1977) 1 BLR 49, in which a Bahamian court decided it was a matter of the parties' intention and that each case would turn on its own facts as to whether the annexation to land was such that the house formed part of the land.

50. Although no legal definition exists, this term is understood to refer to land which has passed down

from generation to generation within the family and by general agreement is not to be sold.

51.   See chapter 10.

52.   See article 38(1) statute of the International Court of Justice.

53.   *Attorney General of Barbados v Jeffrey Josephs and Lennox Ricardo Boyce* [2007] LRC 199 (CCJ), and David Batts, 'The CCJ: Proving Detractors Wrong or Flattering to Deceive' *Caribbean Rights*, Vol. 1 issue 1(May 2007): 3.

54.   See chapter 9.

Chapter 6 – *The Constitution of Jamaica*

1.   See chapter 4 for an account of its creation.

2.   See *CCSU v Minister for Civil Services* (1985) AC 374; and, discussion by Professor Albert Fiadjoe in *Commonwealth Caribbean Public Law*, 3rd ed. (London and New York: Routeledge-Cavendish, 2010), 27–29.

3.   See, for example, *Nerine Small v DPP* [2013] JMSC Civil Full Court 1 (Director of Public Prosecution's decision not to prosecute set aside due to error of law); *Jamaican Bar Association & Others v A-G* SCCA96/102/108 of 2003 (judgment delivered December 14, 2007), (Police seizure of documents and search of law offices breached right to legal professional privilege); *Holness v Williams* (2015) JMCA Civ 21 (Leader of the Opposition exceeding constitutional power).

4.   See *Hinds v R* (1976) 1 All ER 353 (Parts of Gun Court Act struck down as breaching separation of power); and *Julian J. Robinson v Attorney General of Jamaica* [2019] JMFC Full 4, judgment delivered April 12, 2019, (NIDS Act struck down as infringing rights to privacy).

5.   See chapter 9 for limitations on the rights.

6.   Section 13(5).

7.   Section 13(8) and (12).

8.   Section 19.

9.   *Holness v Williams* (2015) JMCA Civ 21 and *Dabdoub v Vaz* SCCA 45/47 of 2008.

10. Section 48(3).

11. A minimum of 11 Ministers must be appointed (section 69(1)). At least 2 Ministers, but no more than 4, must be appointed from the Senate (section 69(3)).

12. Section 64 of the Constitution of Jamaica.

13. See chapter 5, note 4.

14. The judges of the Judicial Committee of the Privy Council commented on the ease with which the right of appeal to themselves may be abolished, in *IJCHR v Burnett* (2005) UKPC 3 and 65 WIR 268, see also chapter 10, note 15.

15. The Minister of Finance and the minister responsible for electoral matters, may not be appointed from the Senate (section 77(1)).

16. The effort to exclude judicial review must be read subject to section 1(9) and the possibility that the court may construe the clause as not being applicable to acts which are ultra vires the Constitution.

Chapter 7 – *The Trial Process*

1.   See chapter 11 for more on the jury system.

2.   Section 13 Crown Proceedings Act.

3.   Defamation claims are the only civil cases usually tried by judge and jury.

4.   *R v Sharp* [1988] 1 WLR 7 at 11F; see also Peter Murphy, *Murphy on Evidence* 7th ed. (London: Blackstone Press Limited, 2000), 196–243.

5. So that, for example, when strictly applied it may be impossible for a person to prove his own age if his mother is unavailable to give that evidence.

6. The caution is a warning that anything he says can be used against the person charged at his trial and of his rights to remain silent; see *The Judge's Rules* [1964] 1 WLR 152.

7. See *Kuruma, Son of Kaniu v R* [1955] AC 197.

8. In the case of *R v Hines* (1971) 17 WIR 326 a Rastafarian was allowed to take an oath to Haile Selassie according to his religious belief.

9. Part 32 Supreme Court of Judicature of Jamaica Civil Procedure Rules 2002.

10. The tradition of trials being held in public is well established in the legal system we inherited. Public observation of trials helps to guarantee fairness; see discussion in *Khuja v Times Newspaper Ltd and Others* [2019] AC 161 on the importance of 'open justice'.

11. The court's media protocol may be viewed at https://supremecourt.gov.jm/content/media-protocol

12. David Batts, 'To Sit or Not to Sit, Contempt or Contrition'. *JAMBAR* Nov 2003 Vol. 11: 1 for a discussion of what constitutes contempt of court.

13. *Ambard v AG* [1936] AC 322.

14. In *Re Maharaj* [1977] 1 All ER 411, the court awarded damages when a fair hearing was not given prior to punishment.

Chapter 8 – *Other Institutions of Governance*

1. Professor Anthony Harriott provides a critical analysis of its structure in *Police and Crime Control in Jamaica: Problems of Reforming Ex-Colonial Constabularies* (Kingston: The University of the West Indies Press, 2000), 26–44.

2.   In *Lennox Gayle v Regina* [2017] JMSC Crim 1(heard February 23, 2017) the police power of arrest was explained.
3.   Section 33 Constabulary Force Act.
4.   Solicitors in England today are allowed to appear in court.
5.   Lawyers qualified in other countries must complete a six months course of study at a regional law school before being eligible to practise law in Jamaica.
6.   See discussion in chapter 9 (under *Role of the Attorney-at-Law*).
7.   Attorneys may also be punished for contempt of court, see chapter 7 (under *Contempt of Court*).
8.   Only public companies which meet the criteria of the Jamaica Stock Exchange are listed on the stock exchange.
9.   Unless the landlord obtains a certificate of exemption from the Rent Board.
10.   The Trespass Act was passed in 1851 as part of the effort to ensure the recently emancipated would continue working on sugarcane plantations. Trespass to land is not a crime in England but a civil wrong (tort).
11.   That is 60 years for land owned by the state and 12 years for all others. See sections 3 and 38 of the Limitation of Action Act.
12.   See *Commissioner of the Independent Commission of Investigations v Police Federation and others* [2020] UKPC 11.
13.   See *In Re an Application for Guardianship of a minor child 'F'* [2016] JMSC Civ 193 for a discussion on adoption and its relationship to the court's *parens patrie* jurisdiction under the Children (Guardianship and Custody) Act and the Child Care and Protection Act.

Chapter 9 – *Rights and the Rule of Law in Jamaican Society*

1. See Anton Hermann-Chroust, 'Fundamental Ideas in St Augustine's Philosophy of Law' *American Journal of Jurisprudence*, Vol. 18, 57, which is contrary to the view of Natural Law theorists such as Thomas Aquinas.

2. At their coronation on April 11, 1688, King William and Queen Mary were by law required to swear an oath to govern the people according to 'the statutes in Parliament agreed on, and the laws and customs of the same'. The country could, by law, no longer have a standing army without parliamentary approval and any such army had to be under the control of Parliament.

3. J. R. Maddicott, in his monumental work *The Origins of the English Parliament 924-1327* (Oxford: Oxford University Press, 2012), traced the origins of parliament to the reliance on advisory assemblies by English monarchs. The grant by King John of Magna Carta (The Great Charter) in 1215 was a significant development. It was however really a concession to rebellious Barons whereby the king promised among other things not to imprison persons arbitrarily and agreed not to impose taxes without the Baron's assent. However, the requirement for approval of taxes was one reason why the assemblies were repeatedly summoned in the years and decades that followed. Its representative character gradually improved and in the year 1237 the first 'parliamentum' to be so called was summoned. Eventually the Parliament consisted, not only of nobles but also Knights, (representing counties), Burgesses (representing town or city dwellers), and also the lower clergy. The Knights and Burgesses were elected representatives albeit on a narrow franchise.

4.   Its lofty ideals notwithstanding, the French Revolution ultimately results in dictatorship when a general in the army, Napoleon Bonaparte, seizes power.

5.   Lincoln's emancipation declaration of 1863 was designed to weaken the ability of the rebellious states to sustain their economy and hence to wage war.

6.   Haitians freed themselves from the yoke of French slave masters by violent revolt and in 1804 became the first free Black state in the western hemisphere; in the process defeating an army Napoleon sent to retake the island, then called Saint-Domingue.

7.   Although the transcript of the parliamentary debates shows there was resistance to their inclusion because some did not want to take away from the supremacy of Parliament.

8.   Jamaica Constitution section 13(2) and see *Julian J. Robinson v the Attorney General of Jamaica* 2019 JMFC Full 4, unreported judgment delivered April 12, 2019.

9.   See *Hemans v Attorney General* [2013] JMSC Civil 75 (unreported judgment delivered May 31, 2013).

10. See chapter 11 for practical examples of the law in action.

11. This statute passed in England in 1676 is an example of a law applicable to Jamaica because it was received due to the principles of Reception of Law discussed in chapter 3.

12. See chapter 5 for a discussion of equity.

13. See chapter 8.

14. The regional law schools are Norman Manley Law School (Jamaica), Sir Hugh Wooding Law School (Trinidad and Tobago), and the Eugene Dupuch Law School (The Bahamas).

15. A judge cannot be made redundant. See chapter 6 for a discussion on the constitutional protection of judges.

Chapter 10 – *International Law, Law Enforcement, and The Caribbean Court of Justice*

1. See William W. Bishop Jr. *International Law Cases and Materials* 3rd ed. (Boston, MA: Little Brown & Co Law & Business, 1971), 1–11, for a definition of international law.
2. Bishop, *International Law Cases*, 12–20.
3. Civilian casualties of the war included 6 million Chinese, 7 million Soviets, 3.6 million Germans, 2 million Japanese; the total dead, inclusive of military and civilian, is estimated to be in excess of 46 million. See Martin Gilbert, *The Second World War: From Casablanca to Post-War Repercussions 1943-1945* (London: The Folio Society Ltd, 2012), 863.
4. The five permanent members are the United States of America, Russia, United Kingdom of Great Britain and Northern Ireland, France, and the People's Republic of China. The veto power given to these permanent members has on more than one occasion prevented decisive action by the United Nations.
5. David Stafford *Endgame 1945: The Missing Final Chapter of World War II* (New York, Boston, London: Little Brown and Company, 2009), 512–15 for details of the punishments administered.
6. The United Nations Charter also refers to human rights in articles 1, 55, and 56.
7. See Patrick Robinson, 'Independence is a Right Not a Gift; Lessons from Resolution 1514 and Chagos Advisory Opinion' in *Eminent Caribbean International Law Jurists: The Rule of International Law in the Caribbean* edited by Winston Anderson, 34–73

(Trinidad and Tobago: CCJ Academy for Law, 2019)
on the role of the United Nations in the decolonization
process.

8. See article 38(1) Statute of the International Court of
Justice.

9. This monumental agreement was signed in Jamaica
which is the designated headquarters of the International
Seabed Authority.

10. See Winston Anderson, 'The CCJ as an International
Court' in *Eminent Caribbean International Jurists*, 394.

11. A Jamaican, Shanique Myrie, was successful in
proceedings brought against the Government of
Barbados, see *Shanique Myrie v The State of Barbados*
[2013] CCJ 3(OJ).

12. As decided in *Independent Jamaica Council for Human
Rights and others v Syringa Marshall Burnett and the
Attorney General* (2005) UKPC3; 65 WIR 268.

13. See, David Batts, 'Judicial Independence, The Jamaican
Bar Association and IJCHR & Others v Attorney
General of Jamaica' *West Indies Law Journal* Vol. 31
May & October 2006: 115.

14. See chapter 5, note 37; chapter 6, note 14, and David
Batts, 'Why the Rt Honourable Mr Justice Michael de
la Bastide P.C., T.C. President of the Caribbean Court
of Justice is Wrong', *West Indian Law Journal* Vol. 32
May 2007: 87.

15. See chapter 5, note 37; Stephen Vasciannie, 'The
Caribbean Court of Justice: The Next Steps', *West
Indian Law Journal* Vol. 35 May 2010: 111; and
Stephen Vasciannie, *Caribbean Essays on Law and
Policy* (Kingston: University of Technology Press, 2020),
198–202.

16. Since the onset of the COVID-19 pandemic, appeals to the JCPC have been heard virtually. This has dramatically reduced, but not eliminated, the cost differential. Documentation still has to be filed and solicitors retained in London to attend to that.
17. *The Caribbean Court of Justice: The First Ten Years* (London: RELX, 2016).

Chapter 11 – *The Law in Action – Questions Jamaicans Ask*

1. *Gayle v Regina* [2017] JMSC Crim 1(unreported judgment dated February 23, 2017).
2. *The Jamaican Bar Association and Others v the Attorney General and the Director of Public Prosecutions* SCCA Nos.96, 102 and 108 of 2003.
3. *Gordon v Det Cpl. Brown [2015] JMSC Civ.199* (unreported 17th January 2014).
4. See the judgment of The Honourable Mr Justice Bertram Morrison considering habeas corpus applications of persons detained under states of emergency, *Everton Douglas et al v Minister of National Security et al* [2020] JMSC Civ 267(delivered September 18, 2020).
5. Section 14(4).
6. See chapter 7 for definition of crime and criminal law.
7. Section 4, Bail Act.
8. See *Gowdie v R* (2012) JMCA 56 and *Gordon v DPP* [2014] JMSC 105 (unreported judgment July 4, 2014).
9. See *Everton Douglas et al v Ministry of National Security et al* [2020] JMSC Civ 276 (delivered September 18, 2020), for discussion of Habeas Corpus.
10. See chapter 3, note 15.
11. His name is also spelt Summerset or Summersett in different law reports. Here I adopt the spelling used

by Steven M. Wise, in his definitive work *Though the Heavens May Fall: The Landmark Trial That Led to the End of Human Slavery* (Boston, MA: De Capo Press, 2006).

12. His name is spelt Stewart in some law reports.

13. See Wise, *Though the Heavens May Fall*, 173.

14. [2004] UKPC 47.

15. It is the lawyer (attorney-at-law) who has a duty to advise and represent the accused person as far as the law will allow.

16. See chapter 7.

17. See Coroner's Act.

18. The repairer's lien is the common law right of someone who has rendered service to retain the items serviced until paid for the service rendered.

19. In *Brown v British Caribbean Insurance Company* [2013] JMSCC Civil 20 the insured was not entitled to recover because on the proposal for Insurance he described himself as a 'mechanical engineer' when in fact he was an auto mechanic. This was a material misrepresentation.

20. See chapter 2.

Chapter 12 – *Crime, Democracy and the Way Forward*

1. Most of the ideas in this chapter were first articulated in 'Curtailment of Individual liberty Not a Crime Solution', *Sunday Gleaner* May 9, 2010; 'Detention without Reasonable Cause Not the Solution to Crime', *Sunday Gleaner* June 29, 2008; 'The only viable Solution to Crime' *Sunday Gleaner* November 16, 2008; and 'Detention without Trial' *Gleaner* September 26, 2003.

2. *Herbert Gayle*, 'Core causes of Jamaica's Violence', *Daily Gleaner*, September 28, 2016.

3. For details of Jamaica's challenges caused by organized crime see *The Political Culture of Democracy in*

Jamaica and in the Americas, 2012, 155–75 edited by Anthony Harriott, Balford A. Lewis, Kenisha V. Nelson and Mitchell A. Seligson https://www.vanderbilt.edu/lapop/jamaica/Jamaica_Country_Report_2012_W.pdf; Trevor Munroe, 'Corruption, Organised Crime and Governance', *West Indian Law Journal* Vol. 36 October 2011:77; Anthony Harriott, 'The Emergence and Evolution of Organised Crime in Jamaica', *West Indian Law Journal* Vol. 36 October 2011:3; and Anthony Harriott, Farley Brathwaite and Scot Wortley, *Crime and Criminal Justice in the Caribbean* (Kingston: Arawak Publications, 2004), 3–7 and 238–63; and the 2016 Report of Jamaica's Economic Growth Council, 'Call To Action' https://cabinet.gov.jm/wp-content/uploads/2017/09/EGC-ADVERTORIAL-5col-x-35cm.pdf4.

4. Reasonable cause is required prior to such interference with liberty, see my per curiam (considered) pronouncements at paragraphs 56, 57 and 58 of *Hemans v The Attorney General* [2013] JMSC Civil 75, and the Police Force Orders published in *Sunday Observer* July 7, 2013.

5. For example, the Suppression of Crime (Special Provisions) Act 1974 (now repealed); section 50 A to F of the Constabulary Force Act; The Criminal Justice (Suppression of Criminal Organizations) Act, and The Offensive Weapons (Prohibition) Act.

6. See chapter 8.

7. Zones of special operations are established pursuant to The Law Reform (Zones of Special Operations) (Special Security and Community Development Measures) Act 2017.

8. When Jamaica's homicide trend is compared with other Caribbean countries, Jamaica stands out for its

extraordinarily high rates over a fairly long period. See Anthony Harriott and Marilyn Jones, *Crime and Violence in Jamaica*. IDB Series on Crime and Violence in the Caribbean, 2016, https://publications.iadb.org/publications/english/document/Crime-and-Violence-in-Jamaica-IDB-Series-on-Crime-and-Violence-in-the-Caribbean.pdf.

9. See, *Daily Gleaner* September 21, 2016 which published Dolby's statistics. The reality may have been higher as the killing of one's own slave is unlikely to have been termed a homicide (if it was even recorded).

10. Jamaica recorded 1,301 killings in 2020 and had the region's highest homicide rate at 46.5 per 100,000 people, according to official data published by the Constabulary Force. The United Nations considers any homicide rate of 10 per 100,000 citizens or above to be an epidemic. Jamaica's total killings marked a marginal decline from 2019's total of 1,339 murders and came as another welcome improvement over 2017's sum of 1,647, extracted from Insight Crime, https://insightcrime.org/news/analysis/2020-homicide-round-up.

11. Carey Robinson, *Fight For Freedom: The Destruction of Slavery in Jamaica* (Kingston: LMH Publishing Company, 2007), 91 and 98.

12. Arnold Bertram, *N. W. Manley and the Making of Modern Jamaica* (Kingston: Arawak Publications, 2016), 16.

13. See B. W. Higman, *Plantation Jamaica 1750–1850: Capital and Control in a Colonial Economy* (Kingston: University of the West Indies Press, 2008), 22–29, and Phillip Sherlock and Hazel Bennett, *The Story of the Jamaican People* (Kingston: Ian Randle Publishers, 1993) 159–62 for general discussion.

14. Carey Robinson, *The Iron Thorn: The Defeat of the British by the Jamaican Maroons* (Kingston: LMH Publishing Company, 1993) gives a graphic account of the Maroon Wars.

15. See Hilary Beckles, 'Caribbean Anti-Slavery: The Self-Liberation of Enslaved Blacks' in *Caribbean Slavery in the Atlantic World* edited by Hilary Beckles and Verene Shepherd, 869 (Kingston: Ian Randle Publishers, 2000) and Verene A. Shepherd, 'Liberation Struggles on Livestock Farms in Jamaica during Slavery', in *Caribbean Slavery in the Atlantic World,* edited by Hilary Beckles and Verene Shepherd, 896 (Kingston: Ian Randle Publishers, 2000), and Robinson, *Fight for Freedom.*

16. See chapter 4, note 21.

17. Edith Clarke, *My Mother Who Fathered Me: A Study of the Families on Three Selected Communities of Jamaica,* rev. ed. (Kingston: University of the West Indies Press, 1999) documents some of this in her renowned study.

18. Lorna E. Simmonds documents the history and growth of Jamaican squatter communities and its effect on criminal activity. See Lorna Simmonds, 'The Problem of Crime in an Urban Slave Society: Kingston in the Early Nineteenth Century,' in *Crime and Criminal Justice in the Caribbean,* 8–34.

19. A former Prime Minister famously declared that politics in Jamaica involved a search for scarce benefits and spoils as recorded by Orville Higgins, 'A New Kind of Political Maturity,' *Sunday Observer,* August 26, 2018. Another political leader said that in Jamaica the person who plays by the rules gets shafted, see Erica Virtue, 'Holness twisted PNP comments-Phillips,' *Jamaica Observer,* November 23, 2011.

20. Herbert Gayle, 'Light on Violence-Urgent Need to Reduce Youth Violence,' *Gleaner*, February 1, 2017.

21. See, for example, Anthony Harriott, *Police and Crime Control in Jamaica: Problems of Reforming Ex-Colonial Constabularies* (Kingston: The University of the West Indies Press, 2000).

22. The Website of the Department of Correctional Services posits 31% as the rate for the period 2015 to 2016.

23. Gordon Robinson, *Sunday Gleaner* August 1, 8, and 15, 2021, and September 25–26, 2021 makes persuasive arguments for change.

24. Per Batts J, In *David Chin v the Attorney General* 2014 JMSC Civil 20 (unreported judgment delivered February 21, 2014).

Works Cited

Anderson, Winston. 2019. The CCJ as an International Court. In *Eminent Caribbean International Law Jurists: The Rule of International Law in the Caribbean,* ed. Winston Anderson. Trinidad and Tobago: CCJ Academy for Law.

Antoine, Rose-Marie Belle. 2006. *Commonwealth Caribbean Law and Legal Systems,* 2nd ed. Oxfordshire: Routledge-Cavendish.

Barnett, Lloyd G. 1977. *Constitutional Law of Jamaica.* Oxford: Oxford University Press.

Batts, David. 2003a. Detention without Trial. *Gleaner,* September 26.

———. 2003b. To Sit or Not to Sit, Contempt or Contrition. *JAMBAR* Vol. 11 (November): 1.

———. 2006. Judicial Independence, the Jamaican Bar Association and IJCHR & others v Attorney General Jamaica. *West Indian Law Journal* Vol. 31 (May & October): 115.

———. 2007a. The CCJ: Proving Detractors Wrong or Flattering to Deceive. *Caribbean Rights,* Vol. 1 issue 1(May): 3.

———. 2007b. Why the Rt Honourable Mr Justice Michael de la Bastide P.C., T.C. President of the Caribbean Court of Justice is Wrong. *West Indian Law Journal* Vol. 32 (May): 87.

———. 2008a. Detention without Reasonable Cause Not the Solution to Crime. *Sunday Gleaner,* June 29.

————. 2008b. The only viable Solution to Crime. *Sunday Gleaner,* November 16.

————. 2010. Curtailment of Individual liberty Not a Crime Solution. *Sunday Gleaner,* May 9.

Beckles, Hilary McD. 2000. Caribbean Anti-Slavery: The Self-Liberation of Enslaved Blacks. In *Caribbean Slavery in the Atlantic World,* ed. Verene Shepherd and Hilary Beckles, 869–78. Kingston: Ian Randle Publishers.

Bertram, Arnold. 2016. *N. W. Manley and the Making of Modern Jamaica.* Kingston: Arawak Publications.

Bishop Jr., William W. 1971. *International Law Cases and Materials* 3rd ed. Boston, MA: Little Brown & Co Law & Business.

Bryan, Patrick E., and Karl Watson. 2003. *Not For Wages Alone: Eyewitness Summaries of the 1938 Labour Rebellion in Jamaica.* Kingston: The Social History Project, Dept of History & Archaeology, UWI.

Carey, Bev. 1997. *The Maroon Story: The Authentic and Original History of the Maroons in the History of Jamaica 1490-1880.* Kingston: Agouti Press.

Chroust, Anton-Hermann. 1973. The Fundamental Ideas in St. Augustine's Philosophy of Law. *American Journal of Jurisprudence* Vol. 18: Iss. 1.

Clarke, Edith. 1957. *My Mother Who Fathered Me: A Study of the Families on Three Selected Communities of Jamaica* rev. ed. 1999. Kingston: University of the West Indies Press.

Codlin, Raphael. 2003. *Historical Foundations of Jamaican Law.* Kingston: Canoe Press.

Dick, Devon. 2010. *The Cross and the Machete: Native Baptists of Jamaica – Identity, Ministry and Legacy.* Kingston: Ian Randle Publishers.

Eaton, John. 1966. *Political Economy: A Marxist Textbook.* New York, NY: International Publishers Co. Inc.

Fiadjoe, Albert. 2010. *Commonwealth Caribbean Public Law,* 3rd ed. London and New York: Routeledge-Cavendish.

Gambrill, Anthony. 2007. *In Search of the Buccaneers.* London: Macmillan Caribbean.

Gayle, Herbert. 2016. Core causes of Jamaica's Violence. *Daily Gleaner*, September 28.

———. 2017. Light on Violence-Urgent Need to Reduce Youth Violence. *Gleaner*, February 1.

Gilbert, Martin. 2012. *The Second World War: From Casablanca to Post-War Repercussions 1943-1945.* London: The Folio Society Ltd.

Glenn, H. Patrick. 2010. *Legal Traditions of the World: Sustainable Diversity in Law*, 4th ed. Oxford: Oxford University Press.

Green, William A. 1976. *British Slave Emancipation: The Sugar Colonies and the Great Experiment, 1830–1865.* Oxford: Oxford University Press.

Harriott, Anthony. 2000. *Police and Crime Control in Jamaica: Problems of Reforming Ex-Colonial Constabularies.* Kingston: The University of the West Indies Press.

———. 2011. The Emergence and Evolution of Organised Crime in Jamaica. *West Indian Law Journal* Vol. 36 (October): 3.

Harriott, Anthony, Farley Brathwaite, and Scot Wortley. 2004. *Crime and Criminal Justice in the Caribbean.* Kingston: Arawak Publications.

Harriott, Anthony, and Marilyn Jones. 2016. *Crime and Violence in Jamaica.* IDB Series on Crime and Violence in the Caribbean. https://publications.iadb.org/publications/english/document/Crime-and-Violencein-Jamaica-IDB-Series-on-Crime-and-Violence-in-the-Caribbean.pdf.

Harriott, Anthony, Balford A. Lewis, Kenisha V. Nelson and Mitchell A. Seigson. 2012. *The Political Culture of*

Democracy in Jamaica and in the Americas, 2012. https://www.vanderbilt.edu/lapop/jamaica/Jamaica_ Country_Report_2012_W.pdf.

Heuman, Gad. 1994. *The Killing Time: The Morant Bay Rebellion Jamaica*. London: Macmillan Education Limited.

Higgins, Orville. 2018. A New Kind of Political Maturity. *Sunday Observer*, August 26.

Higman, B. W. 2008. *Plantation Jamaica 1750–1850: Capital and Control in a Colonial Economy*. Kingston: University of the West Indies Press.

Howard, David. 2004. *Kingston*. Kingston: Ian Randle Publishers.

Hutton, Clinton A. 2015. *Colour for Colour Skin for Skin: Marching with the Ancestral Spirits into War Oh at Morant Bay*. Kingston: Ian Randle Publishers.

Maddicott, J. R. 2012. *The Origins of the English Parliament 924-1327*. Oxford: Oxford University Press.

Manley, Michael. 1983. *Jamaica: Struggle in the Periphery*. London: Third World Media.

Munroe, Trevor. 2011. Corruption, Organised Crime and Governance. *West Indian Law Journal* Vol. 36 (October): 77.

Murphy, Peter. 2000. *Murphy on Evidence*, 7th ed. London: Blackstone Press Limited.

Patchett, K. W. 1972. Reception of Law in the West Indies. *Jamaica Law Journal* (1972): 17.

Report of Jamaica's Economic Growth Council. 2017. Call to Action. https://cabinet.gov.jm/wp-content/ uploads/2017/09/EGC-ADVERTORIAL-5col-x-35cm.pdf4.

Robinson, Carey. 1993. *The Iron Thorn: The Defeat of the British by the Jamaican Maroons*. Kingston: LMH Publishing Company.

———. 2007. *Fight For Freedom: The Destruction of Slavery in Jamaica.* Kingston: LMH Publishing Company.

Robinson, Patrick. 2019. Independence is a Right Not a Gift; Lessons from Resolution 1514 and Chagos Advisory Opinion. In *Eminent Caribbean International Law Jurists: The Rule of International Law in the Caribbean,* ed. Winston Anderson, 34–73. Trinidad and Tobago: CCJ Academy for Law.

Robinson, Tracy, Arif Bulkan, and Adrian Saunders. 2021. *Fundamentals of Caribbean Constitutional Law.* London: Sweet and Maxwell.

Seaga, Edward. 2010. *My Life and Leadership, Volume 1: Clash of Ideologies.* London: Macmillan.

Shepherd, Verene A. 2000. Liberation Struggles on Livestock Farms in Jamaica during Slavery. In *Caribbean Slavery in the Atlantic World,* ed. Verene Shepherd and Hilary Beckles, 896–904. Kingston: Ian Randle Publishers.

Shepherd, Verene, and Hilary McD Beckles, eds. 2000. *Caribbean Slavery in the Atlantic World.* Kingston: Ian Randle Publishers.

Sherlock, Phillip, and Hazel Bennett. 1998. *The Story of the Jamaican People.* Kingston: Ian Randle Publishers.

Shyllon, F. O. 1974. *Black Slaves in Britain 1774.* Oxford: Oxford University Press.

Simmonds, Lorna E. The Problem of Crime in an Urban Slave Society: Kingston in the Early Nineteenth Century. In *Crime and Criminal Justice in the Caribbean,* ed. Anthony Harriott, Farley Brathwaite and Scot Wortley, 8–34. Kingston: Arawak Publications.

Smith, M. G. 1965. *Plural Society in the British West Indies.* Kingston: Sangster's Bookstores Limited in association with Berkley, CA: University of California Press.

Stafford, David. 2009. *Endgame 1945: The Missing Final Chapter of World War II.* New York, Boston, London: Little Brown and Company.

Vasciannie, Stephen. 1996. The Privy Council versus The Caribbean Court of Appeal. Cultural Studies Initiative, Office of the Deputy Vice Chancellor, UWI.

———. 2010. The Caribbean Court of Justice: The Next Steps. *West Indian Law Journal Vol.* 35 (May): 111.

———. 2020. *Caribbean Essays on Law and Policy.* Kingston: University of Technology Press.

———. 2022. Law and the Maroon State. *Sunday Observer,* January 9.

Virtue, Erica. 2011. Holness twisted PNP comments-Phillips. *Jamaica Observer,* November 23.

Watson, Karl. 1988. Amerindian Cave Art in Jamaica. *Jamaica Journal* Vol. 21 No.1 (February to April): 13–17.

Williams, Eric. 1964. *Capitalism and Slavery.* London: Andre Deutsch.

Wise, Steven M. 2006. *Though the Heavens May Fall: The Landmark Trial That Led to the End of Human Slavery.* Boston, MA: De Capo Press.

Acknowledgements

This work would not have been possible without the education my four siblings and I received and for which our parents sacrificed so much in time and treasure. I therefore say thank you to the many quality educators at May 'Teacher' Gilchrist's basic school (Falmouth, Trelawny), the Iona Preparatory School (St Mary), Shortwood Practising School (St Andrew), Kingston College, The University of the West Indies (Mona and Cave Hill), and the Norman Manley Law School.

I am also truly grateful for the professional training and experience acquired as a holiday worker at the Insurance Company of the West Indies, as a practitioner at Livingston Alexander and Levy, and as a Puisne Judge at the Supreme Court of Judicature of Jamaica.

Since 2017, when I started this project, my wife Michele, my daughter Renee, my sons Jordan and Brian, as well as my mother, have been close associates reading, editing, and typing drafts of the manuscript. As it developed I called on others who unhesitatingly gave encouragement and advice. I trust they will not mind my mentioning them by name particularly as I take full responsibility for all the contents of this publication and readily admit that I did not always take the advice given. So, to my brother Neil Fairclough, my friends and colleagues Professor Stephen Vasciannie, Basil

Parker, Rev. Devon Dick, Roger Archibald, Michael Williams, Dr Lloyd Barnett, and Kissock Laing JA, I say thank you.

Much appreciation also to Christine Randle and her staff at Ian Randle Publishers whose tireless work transformed a rough manuscript into the polished work you now read.

Thanks also to the people of Jamaica, land we love, whose history, life and struggle inspired this endeavour.

9 789769 628397